THE

ENTERPRISING

ENTREPRENEUR

Building Your Ladder to
Success

D1411546

Brian H. Kayongo

This book is dedicated to everyone who wants to start a side business and eventually be their own boss. I know what it means to fear, procrastinate, have no capital, etc. But if a boy born in a village in Uganda can build successful businesses in Africa and around the world in spite of those challenges, so can you.

David A Abioye says, "Knowledge impacts power to progress, but it takes STRATEGIC STEPS to make it a reality."

Apply the simple strategic steps described in this book and watch your idea grow from a concept into a reality.

I am excited to see you become the Enterprising Entrepreneur you were born to be.

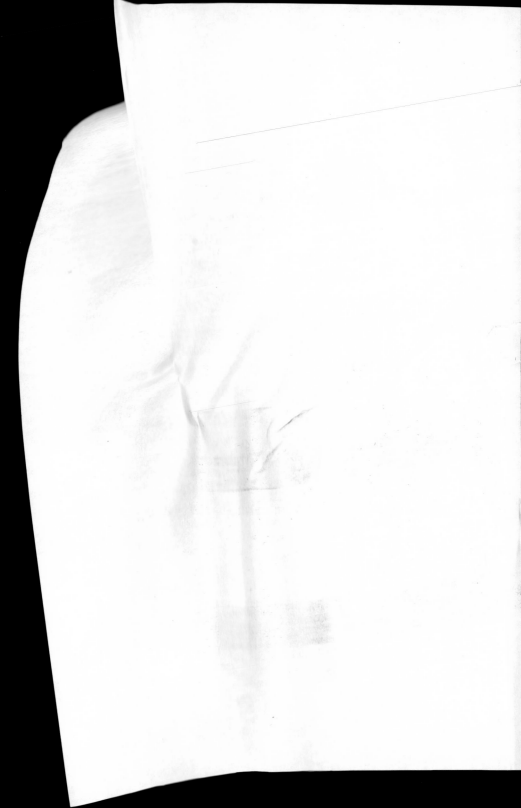

CONTENTS

INTRODUCTION

I BELIEVE, IF you want something done or if you want some change to happen in your life, you have to do it yourself. Don't wait for the government or someone else to bail you out—there are no magic wands or fairy godmothers to come and save you. You are your own magic wand: everything you need to succeed you already have.

The Enterprising Entrepreneur began its formation when a young boy started a chapati (flat bread) business on the hot streets of Kampala, Uganda. Together, we will walk through that young boy's life, and he will show you the lessons he learned, the man he became, and the entrepreneur he is. That boy was me, and this is my story. I am *The Enterprising Entrepreneur.*

I want to use this book to inspire you to take a chance on business, to take a chance on yourself, and most of all, to stop doing nothing and do something. That is when the magic happens. That is when change happens. And it all starts with you. It starts with you developing the muscle to act quickly and make decisions comfortably.

You can create a great future for yourself. It can be done! The steps we will walk through together in these pages will help you to become your own *Enterprising Entrepreneur* and grow your own business successfully.

CHAPTER 1

BACKGROUND: THE YOUNG YEARS

I WAS BORN and bred in Kampala, Uganda, as were both my parents. My dad was a journalist, and my mom stayed at home to take care of the household. In recent years, my parents have become their own Enterprising Entrepreneurs in the field of real estate investing.

Most of my schooling was done in Uganda. I went to Kyengera Primary School and then Seroma Christian High School in Mukono for my senior years. When you spend your youth in a certain place, that place is forged into your heart and stays with you. That is why, even though I have lived in other countries of the world, I will always see Uganda as my home.

After-school activities involved youth leadership roles at the church. Sharing in the hopes and dreams of my fellow youth, who were so full of hopes and dreams, taught me that our future lies in our hands. We can no longer look to the government or our parents to get us jobs. The present and future are our responsibility.

After graduating from high school, I applied for various jobs and finally found a job at Crane Bank during the holiday. I would open bank accounts by marketing to my network of friends from school and church. I was able to work, put food on the table, and pay bills. It was only later in life that I learned we don't have to stay on that paycheck treadmill, but we will get to that epiphany later.

My parents were in the real estate business at that time and often busy with construction. My work on those construction sites with them taught me how to be a supervisor. It is only when you look back at your life that you can see how moments that seemed so insignificant at the time were actually teaching you a valuable lesson you would need later in life. I find that incredible.

Working in the bank taught me a valuable lesson, too, about having respect for other people's hard-earned money. And also, to have respect for my own. Supervising construction projects taught me I could build a life brick by brick in the same way one can build a building. Yet the greatest gift these three jobs gave me was to teach me leadership skills, which I have used often and continue to use to this day.

My First Business

I was sixteen years old when my dad moved from Kampala to the United States. I stayed home with my mom, and the distance put a strain on the whole family. It took my dad longer to settle than he'd initially expected, and the money he sent back to Uganda was not enough to sustain us.

My mom and I had to figure out how best to survive and provide for ourselves. Through months of hard work and tight budgeting, things did begin to improve.

I believe you are always given the solution to your problems. You just have to look for it. As the saying goes, necessity is the mother of invention, and it certainly was for us. My father had given us a mobile phone, so we could speak to him regularly and keep in touch. That very phone would become the solution to our dilemma.

At that time in Uganda in the early 2000s, phones were very expensive. The high service fees and cost of use meant it was too expensive to own. So, it was not as useful a gift as we had all hoped. However, it ended up being our starting capital. We sold the phone and used that money as seed capital (an equivalent of Uganda shillings 320,000) to open kiosk. This kiosk was a little roadside stand that sold a local delicacy—"chapati."

I believe having no money is an excuse. From my experience, you do what it takes to get your idea off the ground. If you must talk to 1,000 people about your idea, do so. If you must sell what you're not using to raise capital to start your business, do so. Have a bias for action.

I wanted us to have a regular income that would ensure we always had food on the table, but I didn't even know how to make chapatis or run a business! I just knew that chapatis were popular, which was a good start. I may not have known how to run a business, but tapping back into my days working with the children at church, my leadership skills were put into action.

I knew I needed a partner in this venture. I learned that a friend of mine from primary school was also trying to find a way to help his family survive. I went to see him and told him I had an idea that might help both of us. He was keen on the idea of working the kiosk and taking some of the profits for the first twelve months.

I only wanted $2 a day per kiosk, which was about 5,000 shillings at the exchange rate at that time. I knew that would go a long way to alleviating our financial problems at home. We started the kiosk, and it was a success! I used the money I was making not only to provide for my mom and pay my school fees (tuition), but also to keep the business growing. A true entrepreneur is never stationary—they are always looking for ways to expand and grow their enterprise.

My target was to have thirteen kiosks. I reached that target. Not all of them were successful, but failure offers its own lessons. Eleven kiosks ran very successfully. From my calculations, thirteen chapati kiosks would mean we could generate enough income to take care of ourselves.

That first chapati kiosk was started because I knew I had to do something to help my family financially, but from that one it developed into a system (chain) of booming businesses. There is nothing more rewarding than to see something you have worked on so hard start becoming a success. I did, however, make a lot of mistakes. As I mentioned, though, mistakes teach us as much as success.

The aim of having many kiosks was to have them be run by someone else. I would take a portion of the profits from each, and, after a year, the person running the kiosk would buy me out. It wasn't all sunshine and roses. Some of the relationships didn't work out, but that was also okay. I missed out on the principles "eyes on, hands on" and "trust but verify."

Sometimes you have to cut ties with people who don't share the same vision or work ethic as you have. It is okay to not be everyone's friend all the time. You have to decide whether you want to be a successful business person or everyone's friend, because you can't be both.

After ten long months of business, my mom and I were back on our feet again. I was just sixteen years old when I started that business, and it taught me that I could take care of myself rather than wait for my parents or anyone else to take care of me. What a great lesson to learn at such a young age!

Life is always going to have hard times. When that happens, you have to decide between two things: *Is it going to break me or make me?* I refuse to let anything break me, so my only option is to let it make me grow and learn.

Journey to America

After a few years, the time came for me to leave for America to join my dad. So, I liquidated all the chapati kiosks and invested the proceeds into real estate, marking the beginning of my passion for this kind of business. When I settled in the United States with my dad, his wish for me was to become a nurse, because it was and still is one of the most lucrative careers here. It was a good, steady job, and there would always be a need for this skill, which meant it offered job security.

I really did not want to become a nurse. It was not a field in which I had any interest at all. He told me many people who come to that country become nurses. It was almost expected of me to follow suit. As is true for many people who have recently moved to a brand-new country, I did not have the means to follow my chosen field of industry or study. I was simply expected to get a job and make a good career out of it, rather than follow my dreams.

We were raised to listen to our parents, and here was my dad earnestly wanting me to go into the medical profession for all the right reasons and with the best intentions for my well-being. I simply could not see myself in that profession, however, and knew I had to speak to him openly and honestly—as hard as that would be. I was raised to listen. I had to follow his wishes, right? Yet I couldn't see myself in the medical profession.

The opportunity came when I was able to sit down and tell my dad how I felt. I explained to him that becoming a nurse was not something I had ever thought of doing; it was something I knew I did not want to do. I wanted to become an accountant. He listened and, as all good parents would, took what I was saying to heart.

He finally replied, "Okay, so how are you and I going to make this happen for you?"

There are times when you look at your parents and think, "Wow! These people just want what is best for me, even if they don't agree with me." Those are special parents, and I am very fortunate to have two who are like that.

THE ENTERPRISING ENTREPRENEUR

I found a community college that we could afford and joined it. I knew I was going to work really hard, so I didn't lose the faith my dad had placed in me by backing my dream. Through this college, I got my associate degree and from there I registered at Framingham State University in Massachusetts, to complete my degree in accounting. I am currently still enrolled there and on my way to graduating with my degree.

I feel as if I can breathe a little easier now that my one goal and dream is coming true. However, I am not one to sit back idly and rest. I always need to keep myself busy in various areas.

While an associate degree is not a great accomplishment compared to what some people have achieved academically, for me it was a solid foundation to which I can return at any time. This qualification gives me the freedom to venture into other areas, as I always have the accounting degree as my safety net in life, which is a great thing to have.

I exhort you to find your own safety net. Venture into any area you want to, but have a qualification that will be your go-to, should you need it. In that way, no matter what happens, you can find a job and earn money. What it also does is give you credibility with people. People respect others who have studied and have some qualifications to their name.

So, go to school, work hard, graduate, get into another area of education—whether it is university, trade school, certification, no matter; just get some qualification. You can then do other things in life, but start with that foundation. It was one of the best decisions I ever made, so I want to stress that point to you.

As I have said, life has tough times, but if you have a qualification, you have something to get you through those tough times. That should be a good motivator.

ক্ষ-ক্ষ-ক্ষ-ক্ষ

Finish what you start.

ক্ষ-ক্ষ-ক্ষ-ক্ষ

THE ENTERPRISING ENTREPRENEUR

One of the great motivators for me to finish my associate degree was I had promised my dad I would work hard and finish what I'd started. For me, that was a big thing. He had put his trust in me, and I didn't want to disappoint him. By finishing what I had started—in this case, the degree—I knew it was a good way to gain his respect. The easy part of anything is the talking. The hard part is the doing.

Beyond my desire to earn my father's respect, I did not want anyone to say of me, "He is the type of person who starts something but never finishes." This, too, has motivated me to keep going and reach the end.

During my associate study, I was also studying IT (Information Technology). I thought this would make me stand out in a future business venture. Don't get me wrong: even though I wanted to be an accountant, the enterprising entrepreneur in me had not died. He was still there, waiting for another chance to start a business.

❦❦❦❦

Find someone you trust to run the business with you.

❦❦❦❦

Around this time, I met my wife, who shared the same vision as I did. We both wanted to make a difference in people's lives and change the way people do and see things. We decided to form a home-care agency with the vision of helping those in need of care and providing a peace of mind. She kept researching ideas and ways of making the business work. We would meet once a week to compare notes. We were learning together and growing our knowledge.

We did not know a lot about running a home healthcare business, but what we did know is we had created this "business kit" to help other people start businesses and guide them in what they needed to do. We decided to use that as our model.

THE ENTERPRISING ENTREPRENEUR

It was a bold move for us, two youngsters taking on a business of that type in a field we were still learning about, ourselves. But we did so much research. We read, we asked, we made notes—every bit of information we could get our hands on, we tracked down and used.

We started the business and still run it today. I was also working for Digital Federal Credit Union, which is a credit bank in Boston. In that way, I was able to feed both my passions, accounting and entrepreneurship.

Loyce, my wife, was working as a nurse at the time, but once we started the business, it took only a month for her to quit her job and start working full time in the home-care business. She was earning a good salary as a nurse, but this business was her dream. She believed in what we were doing. She had asked God about it and felt it was something He wanted her to do.

Due to the business growth, I realized she could not carry it all on her own, so I left the bank and started to work full time with her in the business. We are still working at it, taking all the opportunities we are given and watching our business grow. The business has opened more doors for me as an entrepreneur than I ever would have found working at the bank. The risk was worth it.

I entered into consulting because, when people see you are building something, they want to know how you started and how you built it. It is rewarding to be able to encourage people to grow in their lives. This is the real heart of this book: encouraging people to start something, to support themselves, and to take a chance, because the time is now to begin creating your tomorrow.

I am growing each day, as I have no problem speaking to people one on one, but the thought of speaking to many people fills me with dread. I know I need to grow into this. If I want my message out there, I have to go beyond fear. The question is, do you let fear stop you? If so, what are you doing about it?

ฬฬฬฬ

On the other side of fear lies your breakthrough.

ฬฬฬฬ

I was looking at going into real estate, but I realized, in doing so, I would lose the core of what I wanted to do, which is to teach people, especially foreigners, such as me, how to become an entrepreneur and how to create a life that is fulfilling and rewarding while still being successful and profitable.

I believe everyone can be an enterprising entrepreneur if they want to be, and I am here to help them along the way, to make their dreams come true and ensure they reach their goals. I designed the to help thousands of entrepreneurs remain focused and to finish what they started.

You can preorder your copy of the Entrepreneur Daily Planner now on our website:

www.theconceptenterprises.com

CHAPTER TWO

PLANNING WITH PURPOSE

THE BASES OF ANY success are inspiration and motivation. From there, you need to have a well thought-out and easy-to-execute plan. The purpose of any venture is success. We are going to look at how to create success: from inspiration to execution.

Motivation Creates Movement

The only reason we do things is either because we are self-motivated or because we are motivated by others. Motivation is the key link in any movement.

Motivation comes in many forms, but it all stems from need: The need to feed our family, to change our lives, or to find fulfilment in what we do.

Even when these three things are foremost in our minds, we need to have inspiration in order to formulate an idea. Inspiration comes from researching ideas and speaking to people who have been where you want to go and shown you how that changed their lives.

I have met many people who are unhappy. They are unhappy with their jobs, their relationships, and themselves. They will tell you just how unhappy they are whenever they get the chance.

I always wonder why they don't change their lives, if they are so unhappy. I have pondered this for some time and have come up with the following reasons for people continuing to live unhappy lives.

The reasons I have observed are:

> ➢ Fear of change
> ➢ Pressure from friends and family
> ➢ Financial responsibilities

➢ Doubt in their ability to succeed
➢ Laziness

Fear of Change

Doing anything new is scary. I don't deny that. Consider the time we started the home healthcare business. My wife and I already had good jobs that paid well, so you would think we would have settled or been content. But we did not and were not.

While we were not unhappy with our jobs, we did not feel fulfilled, as our work did not align with our dreams. Therefore, something needed to change.

Pursuing your dream in the presence of fear is a skill like any other. It must be learned and mastered. The more you start doing things that scare you, the quicker you will learn that most of these things are not scary at all. It is our *minds* that cause us to put this stumbling block in front of ourselves. Once we master our minds, we can master just about anything else.

Pressure from Friends and Family

Everybody knows that life comes with unique pressures and stresses. As adults, we have to provide for ourselves. Once we have children, we have to provide for them, too. In many cultures, adult children take care of their older parents and family members, as well. This is a big responsibility to carry.

If you want to make the change from a nine-to-five job to a startup business, the weight of that responsibility will fall heavy on your shoulders. You may even get opposition from friends and family, who will freely remind you about your responsibilities. This may then lead to you stay in the dead-end job that you dread going to every day or may keep you from ever chasing your own dreams. Though you have to be practical, it is possible to balance all of these responsibilities while also going after what you want in life.

When friends and family put pressure on you stay where you are, evaluate why this is. Are they doing it because their lives may get a little harder?

Or are they doing it out of genuine concern for your well-being? Once you have established that fact, you can develop your own appropriate response.

Sometimes, people in our circles don't want us to make changes to better our lives because they are afraid of change, themselves. Watching you make a change can lead them to feel as if they are failing. The answer is simple: This is their problem, not yours. You can encourage them and support them, but you can only live your own life. You cannot make their life changes for them. However, by following your dreams, you may well inspire them to overcome their fear of change and pursue their own dreams.

Financial Responsibilities

There are a number of strategies one can implement to adjust the financial responsibility we have to family and friends in advance of making a career or life change.

First, you need to streamline your finances. It is not easy, but you need to look at whether there are people who depend on you who can actually pay their own way, yet who don't do it because it is easier having you do it for them. They are the first ones to whom you must speak. It may not be fair to expect them to start supporting themselves the very next day. It is, however, fair to give them three months in which to find a job that begins to pays for as many of their needs as possible.

You will then need to look at what you can do until your startup or new venture starts paying you back. Most of us have things we do or buy that we really do not need. The easiest way to cut costs is not to eat out or go to the pub. If you invite your friends to your house, ask that they bring different dishes and drinks. By doing so, you can still socialize while also saving, too.

Remember: this is not forever. It is a personal budget cut that will allow you to follow your dreams. I think a sacrifice is almost always worth it. So, go without delivered dinners. Take public transport instead of driving. Have family activities that don't cost money, such as picnics, museums, or free concerts in the park. Or plan to spend days on the beach instead of indulging in fine dining, movies, and theme parks. When you start saving the little bits, they quickly become big amounts.

Clothing is another thing on which people often spend unnecessary money. Yes, you need to dress well, but it does not have to be designer brands. You can limit your financial expenditures and work out how to pay what you need to pay. This is so important, we will look at it in more detail in the next chapter.

Doubt in Their Ability to Succeed

Self-doubt is such a big obstacle, it deserves its own chapter and will be discussed later in this book. It is worth mentioning here, however, that this is one of the greatest hurdles anyone wishing to change their lives will face.

Many of us have negative thoughts that cloud our minds and steal our confidence, such as:

> ➢ What if I don't succeed and fail dismally?
> ➢ What if people think I am a failure?
> ➢ What if I don't have what it takes?

ക്ക്ക്ക

You will have learned a valuable lesson.

ക്ക്ക്ക

These are all questions that will swirl around in your head when you think about making a life change. The answer is: So what? So what if you don't succeed? No matter what, you will have learned a valuable lesson.

So what if you fail? Failure is part of life. You will sometimes be disappointed, but then you will get up and try something else. And you will keep trying until you succeed. How will you know you don't have what it takes if you never try? How will you know you won't be a success if you don't test yourself?

By limiting yourself and doubting your ability, you will miss out on so many opportunities. Imagine if no one ever stepped out of their comfort zone, feeling too afraid they might fail? We would still be living in caves!

Laziness

Yes, laziness warrants a mention. Some people are willing to make an uneasy peace with living their mere fifty-percent life, because it is just too much effort to make a change. There is very little you can do for these types of people, except to live a life that inspires and motivates them.

Eventually, something will change in their lives, and they will get tired of living their life at half capacity. That's when they will start growing towards becoming the people they can be. That is when they will come to you and ask how you start a business, how you made the change. And that, my friends, is when you can start to work with them and support them in their journey.

Building the Plan

If you want to succeed, you have to build a plan for how you are going to get from where you are to where you want to be.

When Loyce and I began to work together, we designed a business plan that took into account all the thoughts and ideas we had, in order to define the best way to start our business. It contained information about the fundamentals that every business should have:

- ✓ Why is networking important?
- ✓ How do we create a support network?
- ✓ How do we register our business?
- ✓ What resources would we need to get started?

We used this business plan to set up our home-care business. We followed it to the letter, since we didn't know what we were doing, and we grew in knowledge as we grew our business. As time has gone on, I have modified it by adding new ideas and removing concepts I have found to be irrelevant.

When you feel inspired to start your own business, there are some important areas that need to be addressed. Being an entrepreneur is not something you wake up and just start to do, like frying eggs. You need to formulate a well-thought-out plan.

THE ENTERPRISING ENTREPRENEUR

Some of the questions you need to ask yourself and make sure you have clear answers to are:

1. What is your motivation?
2. What do you want to achieve?
3. What milestones will you track to measure success?
4. What capital do you need, and how will you get it?
5. What resources will you need, and how will you afford them: e.g., staff, partners, equipment, office, etc.?
6. What are the running costs: daily, weekly, monthly?
7. How long will your capital cover this?
8. How long, realistically, until you turn a profit?
9. Can you sustain yourself and your business until that time?

Create a budget table like the one shown below. You will be amazed at how many cutbacks you can make.

Absolutes	Necessities
Things you must have:	Things you can live without:
Food	Dining out
Clothes	Going to movies
Shelter	An expensive car
Adequate Transportation	Drinking with your friends
Phone and Internet (usually a must today)	Pampering (e.g., manicures, facials, etc.)

Now, after all this, work out a business plan based on all your answers.

- ✓ Do you need to find capital before you can start your business?
- ✓ If so, how are you going to do that? Are you going to take a bank loan? And if so, can you afford to pay it back?

✓ If you need premises, where can you afford to rent? Or can you work from home until your start-up is established?

Look for premises that are going to suit your needs. Some office spaces come with free Internet. This can save you a great deal of money monthly. Think smart, and be penny-wise.

Write down a timeline. Put where you are now at one end and, at the other, where you want to be in a year's time. In between, mark out milestones that you will need to achieve along the way, in order to get you from point A (where you are now) to point B (where you want to be in one year). To avoid discouragement, make sure these milestones are achievable and realistic.

If your timeline needs to be two years or five years long, that is also fine. Whatever your long-term plans, milestones are going to be your saving grace. Each time you reach a milestone, you will feel invigorated by having achieved one of your mini-goals. This then will motivate you to push on towards the next one.

Milestones are little pats on the back for your perseverance and tenacity.

These are the basics for getting yourself moving. How you make that progress and what you achieve are up to you. This is your dream, your goal, your business. *OWN IT!*

Going for Goals

Setting goals is as important as having a solid plan. If you don't know where you are going, how are you going to plot a path to get there? Keep to your timeline, don't slack off, and work hard. Your goals are only a single journey away from where you are now. Start moving.

I am going to tell you the honest truth: It is not going to be easy. There are going to be times when you want to give up. But if you give up when times are tough, then you will remain wherever you stop and never achieve what you want in life.

Take a breather, but don't quit. Running your own business is hard work and may involve long hours and stress. However, the advantage of running your own business is the freedom of being your own boss, including deciding your own game plan and executing it.

There are few things in this world that can beat the feeling of achievement you get when your business starts to pay its own way. Being an entrepreneur is about breathing life into a vision. It is about creating something that wasn't there before. It is creativity in its purest form.

By answering the questions accurately that I mentioned in the previous section and by sticking to your timeline, you will discover the fuel that keeps your business moving forward. Know where you want to be in a month's time. Know where you want to be in six months' time. Then work, work, work to make sure you get there.

The advantage of hard work is that, while it's not always pleasant to do at the time, once you have achieved what you set out to achieve, you forget about all the hard work that got you there and can enjoy the rewards of your efforts.

Achieving your goals can be broken down into four main sections:

1. Start small, grow large
2. Expect obstacles and prepare for them
3. Be tenacious, positive, and realistic
4. Celebrate the victories, no matter how small

Start Small, Grow Large

I have seen entrepreneurs succeed, and I have seen them fail. There are a few reasons why businesses fail, but one of them is that the person starts too big. They have very grand ideas, but instead of starting small and then growing into a big company, they try to leap from nothing to everything. That often leads to falling flat on your face.

I had the dream of launching thirteen chapati kiosk, true, but I *started* with just one and I grew to owning thirteen. Had I tried, with my limited experience and resources, to start all thirteen at once, I would have failed.

What I learned from owning one, I used to open the second. The lessons I learned from owning two kiosks taught me what to do and what not to do when I owned four, six, and finally thirteen kiosks.

You can grow your business to any size you want, or you can keep it as a single, small enterprise. The choice is yours, but start within the boundaries of your capital, wisdom, experience, and knowledge.

Expect Obstacles and Prepare for Them

Most of the preparation for obstacles is mental. It starts with an understanding that there *will* be storms at sea and your ship *will* take a beating along the way. If you don't want your ship to take a beating, stay in the harbor. Just know, however, that you will have failed before you even began.

Half the battle in overcoming obstacles is coming to terms with the fact that they will appear. Be at peace with the obstacles you don't yet see, and trust that you will be ready for them. Many of these you will be unable to anticipate.

There will be other obstacles you *can* anticipate—finances, production, staffing, premises, customers, and the like. For those, you can work out a plan in advance on how to deal with them. Learn from people who are in the field you want to join. Research the industry, and research any and every obstacle you can think of, finding a way to overcome each of them.

When obstacles come your way, take a step back. A giant boulder in your path, when it is right up against your face, will fill your entire view. However, if you step backwards a little, you will be able to put it into perspective and see it has edges. Once you see the obstacle's boundaries, you can figure out how to get around it.

Don't be afraid to ask for help. Only a fool thinks he knows everything. A wise person understands that he knows something about certain things, but he cannot possibly know everything about everything. Ask for advice, and find a way around the obstacle, because it is standing between you and your next milestone. Getting past it is not an option; it's a *necessity,* to reach your goals.

Be Tenacious, Positive, and Realistic

Tenacity is defined as dogged determination. You show it when you grit your teeth and keep going. You will need that driving force, because there will be times when you feel despondent, when you want to give up. It is only through your determination to make your business work that you will get through those times and keep on growing as a person and as a business owner.

I am a great believer in positivity. I believe you can see the good or bad in every situation, if you look for it. I like to look for the good.

There are some people who take it to the extreme and refuse to see any bad in any situation. They are the people who stay sitting at the dining table, eating their roast dinner, while the Titanic sinks.

There is a lot to be said about positivity, but it needs to be dosed with a realistic point of view. It is one thing to say, "Everything is fine," and ignore the problems in front of you until your business fails. It is another thing to say, "Everything is fine," because you have a plan that is going to save you from sinking.

Be realistic in your expectations both of yourself and of others, as well as of what you can achieve. Be positive about your approach to being an entrepreneur, but always remain realistic about your capacity to achieve physically, financially, and mentally, plus when you may be able to achieve it.

Remember: you are not in competition with anyone else. This is your life, your journey, and your business.

Celebrate the Victories, No Matter How Small

We are often so focused on the end goal that we don't stop to look at what we have already achieved. That is why I love the milestones. They force you to stop and see that you have reached a new level in your journey. They force you to see how far you have come. They can remind you just how many obstacles you've hurdled, how many people you have proved wrong, and how much you have grown in knowledge and experience.

Celebrate the victories, because being an entrepreneur is a wonderful journey, and every step of the way deserves to be celebrated. Your first milestone should be as celebrated as reaching the final goal, as it shows that you allowed your inspiration to motivate you. You created a framework for change and implemented that plan. You have begun your journey as a business owner. That is the joy of being an enterprising entrepreneur!

CHAPTER 3

RESEARCH IN READINESS

THE MORE YOU KNOW, the wiser you will grow. That is a given. Researching your chosen field is paramount for succeeding in it.

There are four key aspect to research and the reasons for doing it:

1. Research for Knowledge
2. Research for Value Addition
3. Research for Business Education
4. Research for Personal Education

Research for Knowledge

As a first-time entrepreneur, it is very unlikely you will know a great deal either about running a business or the field in which you are going to establish your business. Research will give you critical information about your chosen field.

Let us use my chapati kiosk business as an example. The first decision I needed to make was what I wanted to sell. The answer was simple: Something people would want to buy. I think that is the answer any business dealing in sales will give.

As a quick reminder, chapati is a thin, flat, round bread, much like a thick pancake. They are simple, quick to make, and delicious to eat. They are much like a soft tortilla wrap, and for Ugandans, they are eaten with a meal or rolled around beans or stew.

My knowledge of chapati, as for most Ugandans, came from being a child and watching my mother cook them. I would wait eagerly to be allowed to take one of the warm, soft breads and eat it, knowing it would be slightly doughy, slightly salty, and very tasty. I knew they were quick to prepare and make. I also knew that all my friends and family loved them. This was everything I knew about chapati at that point. It was a good start, but there was not enough information to run a successful business.

I would later discover that the following pieces of knowledge would be absolutely critical, as I prepared my business:

> ➢ Who was my target market?
> ➢ What would they buy the most of?
> ➢ What was my ideal price point? *Being profitable, while pleasing my customers and minimizing production costs.*
> ➢ At what time of day would the highest sales occur?

Once I had the initial research and basic concepts together, all I needed to find was a good location. The ideal place would be a spot where I would be visible to the people coming and going from work and also accessible to local pedestrian traffic. I found the perfect spot on a busy street. Tick that box.

THE ENTERPRISING ENTREPRENEUR

I would not be able to run it all by myself, so I needed someone I trusted to run it for me. Good staff is a very critical part of any business. That's why I was delighted when my school friend was interested in joining me.

Here I must add a very important point: Staff will always work better when well incentivized. No one likes to feel like they are just another cog in a machine who is making one person—the boss—money. With this in mind, I established the system whereby I took my 5,000 shillings a day, and he got to keep the rest. That meant the more he sold, after he had covered my fee, the more he could keep. This incentive made my kiosks do well and also allowed my friend to see the fruits of his own labor.

We also agreed that, after one year, he could buy me out. In doing that, suddenly, the person who had no job and no clear future cut out for himself not only had a job, but he had a way of becoming an entrepreneur and owning his own business, too.

Let's recap the key steps of this section, for researching and developing a startup plan for your new business:

1. Research for knowledge.

2. Know your product.

3. Research your target market, and establish whether you have enough customers to support your business.

4. Find out if the market is saturated with your product or if there is a gap in the market for your product. This is critical to your success.

5. Research your center of operations.

6. Work out production cost and selling costs.

7. Ensure that you can cover your costs (these include all overhead expenses, such as rent, utilities, staff, etc.)

8. Ensure you will be able to sell your product at a reasonable market rate that covers your costs and still makes a profit.

9. Find trustworthy staff.

10. Ensure you have enough funds to cover the startup period until your business makes a profit.

11. Establish incentives for your staff from the start.

12. Decide whether to own the business forever or if you prefer to establish a fixed time period you want to own it.

13. If the above business lifespan is for a limited time period, have a plan on how you are going to sell the business, and know the profit you will have wanted to make by that time.

Research for Value Addition

In any business, you have two major aims:

* To make money and dominate your competition.

* To enjoy yourself in the process.

Doing research for value addition is about looking for ways to better your product and run your business. This will give you a competitive edge over your rivals.

Large corporations have entire departments devoted to doing research for value addition. Their only job is to research ways to streamline production and cut costs, while still keeping the integrity of the brand. They also seek to create better ways to sell their products to their customers.

Research around value addition is not something you do once. It is a constant process to keep your finger on the pulse of changes in the market and the needs of your customers. Your product plays a specific role in the market and in your customers' lives. You need to understand that role in order to understand the effect market fluctuations will have.

If you have a high-end product, an economic slump is going to affect your business. This is because, when money is tight, the first thing people cut out of their lives are the luxuries. If you are not in touch with your market, this slump would take you completely by surprise, and the loss of sales would cripple your business.

Keep looking for better and more cost-efficient ways of doing what you are doing, without compromising the standard of your product.

There are a few ways in which you can do research for value addition:

> ➢ Legwork
> ➢ Market Research
> ➢ The Internet

Legwork

Legwork means actually going out and finding information about your potential business for yourself. It entails visiting other businesses in the allied fields, to establish what production resources are available for you to use.

Look into manufacturers, distributors, and producers in similar markets. Spend time finding out what resources you have at your disposal, the costs of using them, and the timeframe needed to produce what you need. This will also tell you if the market is flooded.

If you are not selling a product, bide your time. You will be able to see how many other companies are doing the same.

Investigate every detail you can. What are they charging per hour? Is the market flooded? Or is there a niche role I could play in a valued field?

Market Research

One of the best ways to find out about your potential customers is through market research. You may send people out on the streets of your target area with a questionnaire that relates to your product. Or you may create online surveys and put them on social media.

Either way, you will quickly see if your product or service is:

- ✓ Wanted
- ✓ Needed
- ✓ Priced to sell

Some good ideas may not be viable. This is why market surveys and polls will help you find out if there is actually a market for your business out there.

Even if we know it is wanted, is it *needed*? If it is not needed, is it such a great product or service that people can justify spending money on it?

What price will you charge for your service and/or product? Is it a price people will be happy to pay? Or are you going to have to do a hard sell to move it? Does your entrepreneurial venture have a good chance of success?

These are the questions you need to ask yourself realistically. Just because you think it is a good idea, does not mean it is a viable business idea. By asking yourself the hard questions before you start, you will save yourself time and money further down the line.

By doing market research, you can establish who your target market is, what they want, and what they want to spend on it. Doing an analysis of this data will allow you to see if you are in the right area and at the right price.

There is a good reason why big corporations spend millions of dollars a year on market research and product development: It saves the companies a great deal of money. Social media may be the bane of any teenager's parents' existence, but it does have its uses.

Conducting polls and asking the users to give you insight into your potential product or service can help you streamline, eliminate, or re-think your venture.

Again, it will save you time, which will save you money and stress later on. When you cut corners, you are potentially cutting your future profits, too. So do the legwork, do the market research and polls, and be as informed as you possibly can be.

Research for Business Education

Where I come from, and I don't think it is so different in any other place, if you didn't go to school or you didn't study, people judge you for it. It may not be right and it may not be fair, but that is the way it is. There are very few people who have no education or qualifications in their field who actually make it big.

THE ENTERPRISING ENTREPRENEUR

When you run a business, people expect you to have some sort of formal training behind your name. You wouldn't trust someone who isn't a qualified doctor to operate on you, would you? In the same way, the more your read and the more you study, the more you know.

It is much harder to make it if you don't have some sort of sound knowledge in the form of traditional education behind your name. You have to work doubly hard to gain the credibility you can get from a little piece of paper and a great deal of work.

Education or credentialing may be your step one. Go and study the field you want to work in. Get some sort of credibility behind your name. Then, you can move forward with all the other steps I have detailed.

I have often seen businesspeople with great skill be overlooked and underappreciated because they didn't have some certificate to say they had studied their field. If you can go to university, go. If you can go to college, go. If you can study online, do it. Just get some form of accreditation in the field you want to enter. It is needed, and it will also give you confidence in your business.

Even a business course will help. There are many such courses available online and offered by community colleges around the world.

If you are still in school or busy with tertiary studies, try to get work experience within your chosen field. This will help you see the side of the business you may not otherwise be able to see. All forms of study will provide insight into your field. In that way, you will have more knowledge on which to base your decision about whether this area of business is for you or not.

If you have no choice but to jump in the deep end and start your business, then read as much as you can about the field. Find people who are running businesses in related fields, and speak to them in order to gain insights. Use the Internet to learn all you can about every aspect of your field. It is amazing what you can learn when you start researching!

I have often found myself researching something and then stumbled upon some gem of knowledge I never would have thought to seek out. There is no excuse not to further your knowledge base, as there are many avenues open to anyone who wants to learn.

Every entrepreneur knows that knowledge, a sound financial plan, and a good product are the three legs that hold up a business. Any knowledge you gain that you didn't have before is one more brick in the wall of your success.

Research for Personal Education

Reading and research in the areas of self or personal growth are vital for anyone. We always need to learn more in order to grow as people. Through reading, you can learn new things about life and about yourself, things that will not only help you as a person but will also help your business to flourish.

There are many reasons to read. One is to gain knowledge. This includes reading about other entrepreneurs and how they went about starting their businesses. Another is to uncover practical details of doing what you want to do. The third reason is for personal growth, to support your becoming the person you need to be in order to achieve your dreams.

Here are two very popular books that business people I know have read, as well as people who genuinely want to learn how to get the most out of life:

* *The 7 Habits of Highly Effective People* by Stephen R. Covey
* *Rich Dad, Poor Dad* by Robert Kiyosaki

The fact that you are reading this book means you have a hunger to learn more, which is already a huge positive. Reading other entrepreneurs' stories of how they became successful may illuminate for you areas you may not have thought of before. This may save you from making the same mistakes they did.

Reading books, listening to podcasts, and watching TED Talks can all teach you something.

THE ENTERPRISING ENTREPRENEUR

Motivational books and talks can often boost your self-confidence. They can strengthen your weak areas by showing you ways to work on them, which will bring great benefit to your life. I am of the belief that every bit of information that comes your way has something to teach you. The art is in learning to find it.

Allow yourself time to gain knowledge and to learn from other people's lives. Listen to how others found solutions to problems in life and business. You will quickly discover that those obstacles we spoke of earlier are not nearly as insurmountable as they may seem. The power of knowledge is to create new tools and opportunities to make obstacles smaller or to avoid them completely.

Wise people read, clever people read, informed people read. You should read! You should read, study, and do whatever you can to get a qualification behind your name and to grow as a person.

Life is about personal growth, self-support, and financial success. Applied knowledge is power and can save you time and money. It will mean the difference between success and failure.

CHAPTER 4

START TODAY

BEING AN ENTREPRENEUR used to be viewed as something only certain people could do. I don't accept that premise. Anybody can be an entrepreneur if they do good research, plan well, and have a solid business idea that they then follow.

People often say to me, "Oh, I wish I had my own business!" There is a saying that goes like this: If wishes were horses, beggars would ride. Wishing for something and not doing anything about it will not get you a single step closer to your dream than you are right now.

Procrastination is the thief of success.

If you want something done, you have to start doing it today, not tomorrow. It's time to stop wishing. Instead, turn that wish into a goal and start making it happen.

Waiting for Tomorrow Will Steal Your Dreams

Everybody lives a busy life, so it is easy to put things off to tomorrow. Tomorrow isn't too far away. Putting something off doesn't mean you aren't going to do it, right? It *is* just until tomorrow... *WRONG*!

Leaving for tomorrow what should be done today is the surest way of never achieving anything. In the book *Millionaire Process* by Luis Lunson, there is a quote that stopped me in my tracks:

*Instead of saying I don't have time,
start saying it is not a priority and see
how that feels.*

If something was very important to you, you would start it today. If it's not important enough to do today, however, it probably won't be important enough to do tomorrow.

We will always make time for the things that matter. Somehow, we always have time to watch just one more episode of a gripping series. We always find time to hit the snooze button one last time.

Your actions are showing you that an extra episode of that television series is your main priority. Or that extra hour out with your friends is your priority. But each time you put off something important, such as working out how you are going to become an enterprising entrepreneur, you need to be honest and admit that owning your own business is *not* a priority. This will put procrastination into perspective very quickly.

When you say, "I will do it tomorrow," you may as well be frank with yourself and acknowledge that you are probably not going to do it at all, because that is the reality. In most cases, you are just putting off the hard work. But, in the end, you are also lying to yourself. Ouch! That hurts, right? No one wants to be thought of as a *liar*.

So instead, let's be honest and say you would rather make peace with your mediocre life, including your job that brings you no joy, which means that working for yourself and starting your own business are not a priority to you.

If you concur, admitting where your priorities lie, you may as well also close this book and go back to the couch and your TV. *However*, I guarantee you this book will not stay closed for long!

Each of us is inherently geared to want to grow, to learn, and to chase our dreams. It is not something we choose. It is something that sits deep inside us, and it does not sit quietly, either. It jumps up and down and shouts, wanting to be heard.

THE ENTERPRISING ENTREPRENEUR

No one is happy being unhappy. No one is happy feeling unfulfilled. The desire to find contentment in life will never be quiet, until you stop procrastinating and do something.

These the consistent effects of procrastination:

- ➢ It steals your dreams and goals
- ➢ You lose precious time
- ➢ You miss opportunities
- ➢ Your life becomes stagnant

I know saying that procrastination steals your dreams and goals sounds dramatic, but it really isn't. If you have an idea or a dream and you leave it for tomorrow and tomorrow and tomorrow—which never comes—your dream will die. It will slip through your fingers and become lost to you. Though you may blame many other factors, there are only two culprits: you and procrastination.

Time is something we take for granted. We know everybody dies, and we all only have an unknown but finite amount time on Earth. Yet we squander time as if we have infinite time to live and do things.

I don't like to think of life fatalistically. I would rather exhort you to make the most of each day, as it is a wondrous thing to wake up healthy and alive with a fresh, full day ahead of you in which to start creating your future.

ৰ্জ্ঞৰ্জ্ঞ

Procrastination insults the life you've been given.

ৰ্জ্ঞৰ্জ্ঞ

Ask anyone who is dying, and they will say they wished they had more time to do the things they didn't get to do and to be with the people they love. Be respectful of the life you have been given. You are not here on this Earth by accident. You are here for a purpose: to live your life to the fullest and make the most out of the time you have been given.

Procrastination causes you to miss opportunities that could have changed your life and moved you forward towards achieving your goals. People procrastinate most about taking opportunities, because either they doubt the opportunities' potential to bring good to their lives or they doubt themselves.

It comes back to the "So what?" answer. So what if the opportunity is not what you thought it was? You will have learned something about life and about yourself. That alone ensures that taking an opportunity can never be a failure.

The last point I would like to make is this: If you procrastinate, your life becomes stagnant. Look at what happens to a river that slows down to the point that sandbanks build up. Its flow becomes so hampered, eventually it becomes a series of disconnected rock pools that stagnate, go green, and grow slime.

That is a horrible image, but it is exactly what happens when you stop moving forward. You, a beautiful clear, clean, and flowing river, become puddles of stagnant, green, slimy water. I know which of the two I would rather be.

Now let me ask you this: Do rivers stay tidily within their banks? No, they sometimes flood and make a mess. Do we blame the river? Again no, it is just nature at work.

If you try something and you make a mess of it, so what? Don't stress over it! That's just how nature works. Learn to move on and keep flowing. Don't let procrastination grow sludge and slime on your dreams.

Get Moving Today

The best time to start anything is yesterday. This may not be possible now, but remember that the second-best time to start it is today. When I started writing this book, I sat down and wrote something immediately, because if I had put it off to the next day, I would have been pushing it away and saying it was not a priority. It *was* a priority to me, so I made time for it that same day.

You do not have to do everything in one day, but you do need to make a start at it. Start with writing down your ideas. Then brainstorm about how you could possibly make them happen. Write down what you think the potential positives and negatives would be. Think up a name, where you could work from, and the like. That will give you a starting point. From there, you can begin researching each point in more depth, as needed.

It is so easy to put things off. You can say, "Oh, it is so early in the morning. I will just have a cup of coffee, eat something, and read the newspaper. Then I will begin."

Ten o'clock or eleven o'clock rolls around as you close the newspaper, and you say, "Oh, goodness, where did the time go? It is too close to lunchtime to start anything worthwhile now. I will wait until after lunch."

Two o'clock comes around, and you say to yourself, "Wow! The day is just about gone. I may as well rest today and start tomorrow." So, you leave your dream sitting quietly in the corner, waiting for you to pay it the attention it deserves.

You go to sleep, and the next day you wake up and say, "Oh, it is so early in the morning. I will just have a cup of coffee, eat something, and read the newspaper. Then I will begin..."

You can see where I am going with this, can't you? That is how our dreams grow dusty in the corner, soon to wither and die.

What often happens is that people have an idea, get all fired up, and start to plan. They make lists to get going, but then something else comes along that distracts them. The plans are put aside for a better time that never comes.

If you decide that being an entrepreneur is for you, know that you have to start as though you mean to continue. Later, we will talk more about finding your reason for building the business. This reason is what will give you the fire in your belly, urging you forward when distractions arise. But it all starts with one small step forward.

Start. Do something that takes you one step further *every day*. One step, one step, one step, and soon you will see that you actually have made some progress. A journey of a thousand miles begins with the first step.

Starting Now Gets You One Day Closer to Your Goals

The only question you really need to ask yourself is this: Do I want this or need to do this more than anything else?

If you want something badly enough, you will make time for it. Everything else will pale in comparison to you achieving your goals and doing what is necessary to see your dreams come alive.

Everything you do is that one next step. Every decision you make is another step. Every bit of research you do becomes yet another step.

Start today and do something every day that involves making your entrepreneurial dream come true. Make that your main objective for the day. Even if you have other responsibilities in life, you can surely take at least one hour to work on your own dream. You can even split the time into two half hours a day. However, I believe you'll find, once you start moving forward and getting your proverbial ducks in a row, you will want to spend more and more time on your plan.

Think back to one year ago. What were you doing? How were you feeling? If the answers are pretty much the same as you are doing and feeling right now and if you are not feeling fulfilled and happy, then clearly you need to do something else *right now*!

Try this exercise for me, but mostly for yourself.

Take a Post-it Note or a square of paper. On it, write today's date.

Now, write down your job and how it makes you feel.

Below that, write your general state of mind: happy, indifferent, bored, unhappy, etc.

And below that, write what you would most like to be doing in life.

Now stick it on your refrigerator. Every single time you open the door to your refrigerator, you are going to see those words.

Watch how your feeling of discomfort grows as the weeks pass and then the months pass and nothing has changed in your life.

If you still have that note on your refrigerator one year from when you wrote it, write another one and stick it below it.

Those notes are a daily reminder that your dreams are as stuck as you are.

Imagine how incredible you will feel, however, one year after writing that first note, when you write your second note:

Job: *Entrepreneur and owner of my own business.*

Feeling: *Proud of myself and loving life.*

What I most want to be doing: *What I am doing now!*

Wow! Would that not be amazing?

The power of your future lies in your hands, in your mind, and in your heart. It is up to you and only you.

If you are waiting for the perfect time, I can tell you right now there isn't one. You will be waiting until you are on your deathbed.

If you are waiting for someone else, stop. You cannot put your dreams in the hands of someone else. Be your own dream master.

If you are waiting for money to come in, it is not going to fall from the sky, so stop waiting. Find a way, make a plan, and work out how you are going to get the finances you need to start your business.

If you have to start smaller than you originally wanted to, start smaller.

If you have to earn less, budget better.

If you need more time, stop waiting. Use the time you have and use it wisely.

THE ENTERPRISING ENTREPRENEUR

I can't stress enough how all of this—your dreams, your goals, your today, your tomorrow, your future—is in your hands right at this moment. Wasted time and procrastination will steal your dreams faster than you can blink.

If you want it badly enough, you will make it happen. It is that simple.

CHAPTER 5

BACK YOURSELF

IF YOU DON'T BELIEVE in yourself, you cannot expect anyone else to believe in you.

People who come across as believing in themselves do better than those who sound unsure of themselves. When you speak to a person who sounds as if they don't know or aren't sure what they are speaking about, it makes you doubt them. They might know perfectly well what they are talking about, but, without self-confidence, they will come across as not having knowledge or not believing what they are saying.

In business, you need to know what you are speaking about. You need to know your product and/or service inside and out, so you can confidently promote it to your potential clients.

There are three main ways of learning to be confident within yourself. These are:

1. Self-Belief: A Sure Footing
2. Know You Can and You Will
3. Projecting Self-Belief to Motivate Others

Self-Belief: A Sure Footing

If you believe in yourself, you will go forward boldly, because you know you have what it takes to succeed. Self-belief is not arrogance. Rather, it means knowing your strengths and knowing you will use them to succeed.

When you speak to a person who has experience about an area or field, they will speak confidently about it. They have a good base of knowledge to draw from.

Often, when we start a business, we don't have a wealth of experience to draw from. That is when the self-belief kicks in. It doesn't matter if you don't have ten years of experience. You do know you have what it takes to get that experience and right now. You have belief in what you are promoting. And you have belief in yourself that you are going to make it happen. If you don't believe in yourself and what you are doing, how can you expect others to invest money into it?

Self-belief is knowing that, while you may not know everything, you are learning and growing as you gain experience. If you believe in your ability to succeed, everything else falls into place, because you are backing yourself for the win.

The worst enemies against your own self-confidence are:

> ➢ Comparing yourself to others
> ➢ Expectation of perfection
> ➢ Fear of failure

Comparing Yourself to Others

This is something we all do but know we shouldn't. Whether it is a sibling, a friend, a parent, or people we have read or heard about, we find ourselves comparing what they have and what they've accomplished in life against our own life. Invariably, since we have already made up our minds subconsciously to come in second by comparison, we do!

We set ourselves up to fail mentally when we compare ourselves to others. You cannot compare yourself with anyone else, because no one else is you. You think differently, work differently, and have different ideals and goals than everyone else.

Comparing yourself to others just undermines your self-confidence, because it sets a bar of unrealistic expectations for yourself. You can't achieve what Joe Soap did, because you are not Joe Soap. However, you *can* achieve what you have achieved or are achieving, because you are you.

You don't know that person's story or what it took for them to get where they are. Remember: you don't get to see the lead-up to the success. What we tend to do is compare our worst moments in our own lives with the best moments in others' lives.

Have you ever looked at people's social media posts? Those are life highlights. You never see a post where people show their children fighting, their car being repossessed, or their boss shouting at them. Then you sit there and compare their amazing moments with your life's worst moments and think they are equal.

Comparing yourself to others is a waste of time. Instead, compare yourself to who you were yesterday or last year. Use your growth as a yardstick to encourage you to better yourself. The only person with whom you are in competition is whomever you were yesterday. You're in competition with the person you want to be tomorrow.

I will leave you with this lovely little gem from Albert Einstein: "Everyone is a genius, but if you judge a fish on its ability to climb a tree, it will live its whole life believing it is stupid."

Expectation of Perfection

We humans are really hard on ourselves. We expect a lot more from ourselves than we expect from others. Also, we are our own harshest critics. There is very little in life that is perfect ,yet we expect our lives to be so, and when, inevitably, something goes wrong and creates a crack in that illusion, we are devastated.

We tell our children to "do their best," but we don't tell them to be perfect. Yet we tell ourselves that our best is not good enough—we *have* to be perfect. Somewhere along the line, our expectations of ourselves have become warped.

It is okay not to be perfect. It is okay to be flawed . It is okay to be human.

What an expectation of perfection does is it gives us an out so we can accept failure. If we create this very high standard and don't meet it because we cannot, we have given ourselves an "out" in anticipation of failure, even before we begin our new project. Then we can then say, "Oh, I'm not perfect, so failure was inevitable."

However, if you set yourself milestones along your business path that are realistic, should you not achieve one or more of them, it is not because you are imperfect. It is because you did not do what you needed to do in order to reach that particular milestone.

Even though you know you *could* have done it, you chose not to. Your "out," however, must be taken away. So create an expectation of progress, not one of perfection.

Fear of Failure

Sometimes, because we are so afraid of failing, we don't start anything. Our self-doubt lists reason after reason why you shouldn't do something.

Self-doubt has a very loud voice, and it loves to make itself heard. It will tell you that you really shouldn't start your own business and become an entrepreneur because:

- ✓ You have a good job . Why throw it away?
- ✓ Your parents will be disappointed in you for not using the degree they paid for.
- ✓ Your friends will think you are crazy.
- ✓ You don't have what it takes to make it.

Understand: You are going to fail. And there you have it—the word that strikes fear into our hearts and renders us stagnant in life. *Failure.*

I want to tell you that the majority of people who have made it in life have failed time and time again. You should never be afraid of failure. It is just a difficult lesson that will make you stronger and wiser. In addition, it should make you even more determined to succeed.

You should be afraid of not trying. Quitting before you give yourself a proper chance to succeed will sabotage your dreams. Hitting a bump and falling off your bicycle is no reason to throw the bicycle away. Get up, and get moving.

The people who are willing to give anything a go often succeed in many things because they know, even if it doesn't work, it will be an educational experience and there is always something else to try. Or perhaps they are willing to try again and see if it works the next time. They can do this because they don't have a fear of failure. They accept the wins *and* losses as part of life; failure does not hamper their life experience.

You know what I am going to say about failure... So what? It is part of the human condition. Everyone fails at something. There are brilliant athletes who can't sing, corporate CEOs who can't tap dance, and fish who can't climb trees. Each one of those would fail, if they tried.

Find what you are good at. Then, even if you fail, your confidence and determination to succeed will light you up, so you can try again and again—until you succeed.

Learn to address your self-doubt directly. See it for what it is: fear of failure. Then set your mind to carry on anyway. What is the worst that can happen? You fail. Then you try again. Is that the end of the world? No. It is an obstacle to learn from, to move around or over or under, and then you carry forward on your path to achieving your dream as an entrepreneur.

You cannot let self-doubt stop you from living your best life and creating the future of your dreams. That is like shooting yourself in the foot on the morning of a marathon and then saying you can't run the marathon because you are injured. Most of our inability to succeed in entrepreneurship—and in life, for that matter—is self-inflicted.

No one is out to get you. They don't have to be. More often than not, we do a good enough job of hampering our lives ourselves. I am telling you this so you can identify it for the self-doubt that it is and then move onwards and upwards from self-doubt to success.

Know You Can and You Will

When you doubt yourself, you second-guess every decision you make, and this leads to failure. If you believe you can do something, you will act in such a way as to create success. You will project confidence in yourself and your product, which will open doors for you.

Reasons you doubt your ability to succeed:

> ➤ Childhood conditioning
> ➤ Past failures
> ➤ Present pessimists
> ➤ The Human Guilt Factor

Childhood Conditioning

Children who grow up with parents who constantly tell their children they are lazy, useless, and won't amount to anything produce one of two types of children:

* ✶ Those who don't try anything, because they have been conditioned for so long to believe they are useless, or
* ✶ Children so determined to prove their parents wrong that they push themselves to the point of destruction to do so.

Neither is a good scenario.

In an ideal world, parents would love, support, and motivate their children to follow their dreams and not fulfill their own dreams vicariously through their kids. However, we all come to adulthood carrying some childhood baggage. Whether it is a parent or a teacher, there is often someone in our lives who wanted us to be something different than we wanted to be for ourselves.

Accept that it is okay for others to have expectations of us, but it is also okay for us not to meet those expectations. You are not obligated to fulfill any dream and vision for your life but your own.

Read that again.

❦❦❦❦

You are not obligated to fulfill anyone's dream for your life.

❦❦❦❦

Remember how my dad wanted me to be a nurse? Being a nurse is a good job. It is a vital job. We need nurses. However, it was not something I wanted to do. I had to take that expectation my dad had for me and leave it at his feet, so I could pick up my dreams and explain to him why his dreams for me and my dreams for myself did not match.

I am very fortunate that I have a father to whom I can speak; one who listens to my heart and is proud of me. Not everyone has that. You may have to choose between your dream and someone else's dream for you.

It can be hard, but if the person loves you, they only want to see you happy, so they should be supportive of you doing what you've always dreamed of doing.

Being an entrepreneur is something to be proud of. Finding a niche market, creating a business out of nothing, and then making it work—that is amazing. It is admirable. Anyone who does that deserves to hold his or her head up high.

Present Pessimists

When you decide to go after your dream of becoming an entrepreneur, expect some negative input and take it for what it is. Success makes stagnant people uncomfortable, and this discomfort will be expressed out as negativity towards you.

Don't let that stop you! You are following your dreams, and that is all that matters. You can try to explain to them why you are doing what you are doing. You can detail your plan for them and describe how you are going to execute it, so as to give yourself the best possible chances at success. This engagement may even motivate them. Alternately, they may doggedly stick to their stagnant state. That is up to them, of course: their journey is not your journey.

I want to give you some concrete reasons why you should never doubt your own ability to succeed:

✓ No one else is you
✓ Your inspiration is your motivation
✓ You are strong, resilient, and resourceful
✓ Success is achievable by everyone

No One Else Is You

What a great thing it is to be unique. No one thinks like you do. No one has your strengths. And no one can change your life but you.

Your uniqueness is what is going to bring that extra-special something to your business.

Perhaps you are very good with people. Perhaps you have a strong business mind. Or perhaps you are very financially savvy. Perhaps you are tenacious and determined. You may be one of those people who thinks on their feet and can find solutions to problems quickly and efficiently. Whatever it is that makes you unique is going to be your greatest asset.

The field you have chosen along with the business you decide to open and run all stem from your unique strengths. What a powerful thing this is to have at the center of your motivation! You can do it because you have what it takes simply by being yourself.

You may have to improve in those areas of business in which you are not yet strong, but there will always be something that comes easily to you. *That* is your strong point and your go-to, when you need it.

Your Inspiration is your Motivation

The idea that inspired you to become an entrepreneur, whether it was a need or a desire, will keep you motivated to continue, when the going gets tough. It will be the flame that warms you when you need it.

Always remember what your motivation is. Remember the inspiration for why you wanted to start your business. It will carry you on when you are tired. It will be there when you celebrate your milestones. And it will shout the loudest when you succeed.

You are Strong, Resilient, and Resourceful

Life is full of ups and downs, and so is business—for everyone. Once you accept that and don't feel as if you are being singled out and victimized, you will find that you feel better about any obstacles you encounter.

You can do this! You are strong. Otherwise, you would not have had the courage to start.

You are resilient. Otherwise, you would not have had the strength to stay on the course.

You are resourceful. You will find a way past any obstacle, because you know there is a solution to every problem, and you have honed your research skills to such an extent that you will be able to find it.

Success is Achievable by Everyone

There is no reason for you not to be a successful entrepreneur. Success is not selected only for a special few. *Everyone* can be successful, if they plan well, work hard, and keep going.

We often think, mistakenly, that success and happiness belong to others, and that we are not meant to have them. This is nonsense. There is no discrimination where success is concerned. You may have to work hard, you may have to work long hours, and it may take time, but success is there at the end, waiting for you.

Projecting Self-Belief to Motivate Others

If you meet people and can confidently speak about your goals with knowledge and self-belief in what you are saying, you will find that it motivates other people. In any business, you need to have the support of other people in many areas. That is why being able to project your self-confidence while also supporting yourself is so important.

Back yourself. Accept that you may not be perfect, but you are determined to make this work. Back yourself by knowing, if you hit a bump and fall down, you will get up and try again.

Do this for yourself and you will see that others are motivated by your actions. If you are confident within yourself, confident about the potential of your business, and confident about your product, you will see how this attitude draws people to you.

Self-belief will get you far in business, as people like to support people who believe in their product and in themselves. Projecting faith in yourself will boost your confidence and bolster your strength, even when you are feeling discouraged.

Things change, so bad times will invariably become good times soon enough. It is not worth throwing in the towel just because things are not going well at the moment.

Projecting self-belief will help you around others. Being positive about what you are doing goes a long way in making others feel positive about what they are doing for you. Believe in yourself and others will, too.

Here are some strategies for how to project self-belief:

* Choose to be an optimist
* Embrace being human
* Use your strengths
* Create a support system
* Find a mentor

Choose to be an optimist

It's easy to be pessimistic. There is always something going on in life that can make you feel down. The trick, however, is to say, "Yes, this happened, but look at all the good there is in my life."

Focus on the good and on what you can change, then let the rest go. If you can't do anything about it, let it go. If you can do something about it, do it.

Embrace being human

As I said in the previous section, humans are fallible. We mess up; we make mistakes. That is just what we do sometimes.

We also do great things. We create amazing and successful businesses, employ people, and give others the opportunity to get a start on creating their dreams and reaching their goals.

There is a lot more to being human than just dealing with the negatives. It is a great gift to be here, right now, wanting to become an entrepreneur.

This is the best time for entrepreneurship. The world has made a mental shift about people owning their own businesses. Many people are finding that larger companies even like working with small businesses. There are tax cuts for SMEs (Small to Medium-size Enterprises) and other benefits, which you will learn about when you do your research.

Use your strengths

Embrace being human in all its forms. Don't judge yourself for your lack in some areas. Instead, celebrate your strengths while you work on your weak areas. Do research, ask questions, and learn how to limit the impact of any weaknesses or deficiencies in your life.

Your strengths are what will bolster you when you feel you can't go on. That is why creating a positive attitude about life is imperative. You *can* do this. You *do* have what it takes. And you *will* make it.

The strength you have is your belief—and mine, too!—in your ability to make being an enterprising entrepreneur work for you. You know what your strengths are. Use them to their fullest to give you support and uplift you, as you go along your journey.

Create a support system

When you are having a bad day, it is always good to have someone to speak to who can lift your spirits and tell you to hang in there, as it will all work out in the end. In business, it is good to have that same support system.

Networking with like-minded people, especially entrepreneurs, will help you in tough times. They will celebrate your victories with you, as they are going through the same journey you are. They will understand where you are coming from better than anyone else.

We will speak more about networking in a later chapter, but it is important to mention it here, as it is an important part of being able to project self-belief.

Find a mentor

A mentor is someone with experience who is willing to guide, share with, and support you on your own journey.

This is usually someone who has been in business for many years, so their knowledge and abundance of experience is invaluable.

If you don't know of anyone, go to conferences allied to your field, and ask around. Don't be shy to ask for help or say that you are still learning. Every self-made person started where you are now, and they should be willing to give you guidance and support.

ങ്ങങ

In summary

* Do your best, and accept that there are going to be ups and downs. Don't let those downs stop you from continuing on your journey.

* Keep to your plan, work towards your milestones, and surround yourself with positive, like-minded people. Keep a positive outlook, and see the long road, not the obstacles.

* You *can* become an entrepreneur, so keep your chin up and your shoulders back, and be as prepared and as positive as you possibly can be.

CHAPTER 6

COMPOUND EFFECT IS COMPOUNDING

THROUGH MY ACCOUNTING studies, I have learned that money invested in an account with compound interest grows faster than money invested in an account with simple interest. I will explain why this is and why this is more than just a simple lesson in accounting. This is, in fact, a very sound lesson the pertains both to business and to life and illuminates how to maximize the impact of your daily habits.

The Basics of Compound Interest

Compound interest occurs when your initial investment amount incurs interest; after that, future interest is calculated not only on the initial amount but on the initial amount plus the interest.

This means that if you invest $100 at ten-percent interest, you will get $10 of interest on that money. With compound interest, your next interest payment would be calculated on $110, which would accrue $11. The next recalculation of interest would then be on $121 and accrue $12.10, making your initial investment quickly grow to $143.10. You can see clearly how your investment can grow in a short time, certainly as compared to receiving interest only on the initial amount over and over.

The graph below shows you how much more you get out of this Eighth Wonder of the World:

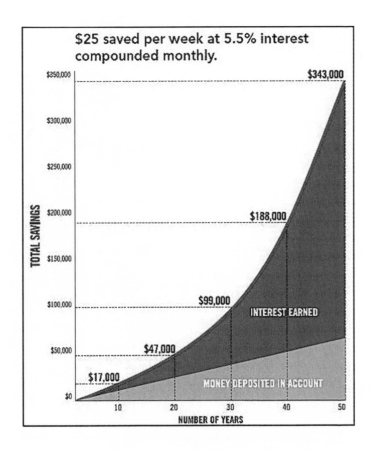

In the same way that compound interest works in the financial world, your compounded investment—i.e., your time and effort—will escalate in a similar or even far greater way.

How to Compound Effort to Create Greater Growth

When you put effort and time into something, the effects compound and grow exponentially. When you start your business, your knowledge and experience are limited, so your growth will be small and slow.

Don't lose heart! As time goes on, your knowledge will grow and so will your experience. That is when the compounding magic begins. You can do more things in less time, and each of those things will have a ripple effect that will reach more people and create more income.

As you grow and learn, you will find new avenues opening up to you. The more you know, the faster you will grow. Focus on what you are doing, give it your time and effort, and then watch it grow.

You cannot expect to open your business and be a super-success on day one. But by working smart, keeping focused, and yes, working hard, all those days of hard work will begin to compound and turn into something great.

Let's look at how this works in life. You know those days when you are in a bad mood about one thing, and everything seems to go wrong? Well, say hello to compound interest spreading that negativity into your life.

In the same way, when you look for the positive things around you and happening to you, choosing to focus on them instead of on the negative, more and more good things will become visible and happen for you. Compound interest happens in life, whether you accept it or not. You can decide, just as every hero has had to decide, whether you are going to stay on the dark side or not.

I would rather compound good in my life than negativity. You can, and should, use the compound effect in every area of your life. If you want to change your health, start today with something small, and keep adding a new small thing each day.

Perhaps, today, you drink an extra glass of water. Perhaps, tomorrow, you go for a walk in the park, and the next day you take a yoga class or cook a nutritious dinner, instead of eating out. If you keep doing one small thing every day, the effects on your health will improve dramatically over time.

One change, one step at a time. Each day will compound and grow. You may be busy and your life may not leave you with a lot of time, but you can always take one hour a day to move yourself towards creating your business.

If circumstances don't allow for you to leave your current job, it doesn't mean that you have to shelve your business idea. It just means you have the time to work on your plan, do your research, and save and create capital, so you'll be ready when the time comes to start your business.

Saving to Create Growth

If you want to start a business, you need capital. For me, I used the money from the phone we sold as my capital investment.

You will have to look seriously at what capital investment you will need and how you are going to get it. Perhaps you have something to sell. Perhaps you have money to start with. But, for most of you, this means you either have to borrow money from a bank or save for your capital investment.

If you are going to borrow money, either from a bank or from an individual, make very sure you know how long you have to pay it back, what interest rate they are going to charge, and what the payments must be. Only then can you decide whether you can really afford to borrow the money.

Many people get really excited about getting a loan, as it means they are one step closer to starting their business, but they don't do the research into what their repayments are going to be. They use the money and then, when the business is slow to start, they find they cannot pay back the required installments. This forces them either to borrow from someone else to pay the first loan or to close their business altogether.

If you can't afford to pay it back, don't borrow it. It is that simple. Instead, find another option. Start saving, for example.

THE ENTERPRISING ENTREPRENEUR

Take a percentage of any money you are bringing in, and put it into a separate bank account. Do not try to save by using the same account you use for day-to-day purchases. That is the fastest way to spend your supposed savings! And remember how much faster your money grows when you place it in an account that offers compound interest?

You may have to work at a job you are not completely happy with for a while, in order to save to start up the business you want to build. In this world of instant gratification, you may have to wait. We live in a time where you can have anything delivered to your door or find anything you want at the click of a mouse button. Food, clothes, entertainment, furniture—you name it, it can be delivered.

We are the Now Generation, and it can be difficult to want something such as owning your own business and not be able to have it *right now*. But learning to save for what you want is not a bad thing. It is actually a very good thing, as you will appreciate every little bit of money you have and will use it much more wisely.

Save a little every day, and it will grow. The doubling-penny effect demonstrates this very well.

On the first day of the month, you have one penny. On day two, you have two pennies. If you keep doubling your pennies each day, would you believe, after thirty-one days, you would have over $5 million?

Check out the image on the next page:

Day	Value
1	$ 0.01
2	$ 0.02
3	$ 0.04
4	$ 0.08
5	$ 0.16
6	$ 0.32
7	$ 0.64
8	$ 1.28
9	$ 2.56
10	$ 5.12
11	$ 10.24
12	$ 20.48
13	$ 40.96
14	$ 81.92
15	$ 163.84
16	$ 327.68
17	$ 655.36
18	$ 1,310.72
19	$ 2,621.44
20	$ 5,242.88
21	$ 10,485.76
22	$ 20,971.52
23	$ 41,943.04
24	$ 83,886.08
25	$ 167,772.16
26	$ 335,544.32
27	$ 671,088.64
28	$ 1,342,177.28
29	$ 2,684,354.56
30	$ 5,368,709.12

That is the power of compound interest, whether you use it in business, savings, or life. This metaphor is from Darren Hardy's book, *The Compound Effect*.

Be conscious of the compound-interest effect in your life. Every decision you make, everything you say, and everything you do all work through the principles of this effect.

If you put in nothing, you will get a whole lot of nothing back.

If you put in negativity, you will get a lot of negativity back.

If you put in a small amount of effort and money every day, however, you will find that it compounds to the point where you have a lot of both.

However, it all starts with you. What will you choose to compound in your life?

Using Your Compound Effects to Help Others

Someone once told me that you can't help everyone, but you can help someone. They told me, if we each help two people and those two people help two people, the compound effect would soon reach across the world.

I am a great believer in giving back. Giving back does not always mean financially. It means giving back your time to your parents, who gave so much of their time to you as a child. It means giving back to the school you attended as a child, by helping them where you can. It means giving back support and time to the friends who supported you during your years of friendship. It means giving back to your community in the form of charitable acts.

There is a movement called the DoT Movement. DoT standing for "Do One Thing". The man who runs it is Braam Malherbe, a South African and extreme adventurer.

Braam started a movement using the premise that everyone doing just one thing could make a difference in the world and help the sustainability of the Earth. He says, if each person on the planet does just one thing, that makes seven and a half billion "one things" being done. Seven and a half billion changes can truly change the world!

In the same way that the doubling of pennies exponentially leads to great sums of money, the doubling of kind acts leads to great sums of joy and happiness in the world. If you are the first penny and you help someone, beginning the cycle of repetition, it compounds in such a magnificent way that, after a month of everyone helping others, over ten and a half million people can be helped—all starting with one simple act done consistently.

We all know someone who needs a little motivation or some time spent with them. It could be fixing your mother's creaky front door. It could be taking your grandmother out for tea. Or it could be spending an hour at a youth center, coaching basketball . Just do one thing, and ask the person to pay it forward. In that way, we can spread kindness and good into a world that seems intent on selling us only the bad.

The "I Don't Have Time" Syndrome

When I speak to people about doing one thing so it can compound from something small into something great, a lot of people tell me they think it is a great idea.

But then, whether it pertains to savings or helping people, they are often quick to follow up that thought with the greatest lie we tell ourselves: "I don't have time." They say they think it is a great idea and they wish they could do it, *but* they simply don't have time.

I'd like to challenge everyone on that. I do not believe most people (sure—there are always exceptions) can't find an hour to spare in their day. What about that hour you spend on social media? What about that hour you spend watching a TV series or going out with a friend or napping?

Cut down your time on anything that is not helping you get from where you are to where you want to be. They are hollow time-wasters.

I am not saying you can't ever socialize or go on social media or watch TV. What I am asking you to do is to be honest about what you *really* mean when you say you don't have time. It's this: "Changing my life is not a priority to me."

If you can live with saying that to yourself, then continue to lie on the couch and watch TV all day. Just don't expect your life to be any different a year from now than it is right now.

If you really don't have time during the day, take an hour out when you get home. Wake up an hour earlier, or take an hour out of your weekend. Take that hour and use it to start compounding the change you want to make in your life. Just don't tell me that you don't have time. If it is a priority, you will find time.

Do it for yourself, for your business dream, and to give back and create a better world. Just one hour, just one penny, just one person taking consistent action—that is all it takes to revolutionize your life.

CHAPTER 7

FOCUS CHANGE AND ADAPT

IF YOU ARE NOT focused, you will achieve very little, as anything and everything will distract you. It is easy to be distracted, and there are a thousand things that will try to distract you. However, you need to prioritize what you are doing and tell yourself that this is the most important thing right now. Everything else can wait.

If it is important enough to do, it is important enough to give it your full attention.

Focus can be broken down into two categories:

➤ Focus for research and planning
➤ Focus for development and input

Focus for Research and Planning

In this day and age, it is very easy to be distracted. You may sit down to work on your business plan or plot your next move forward in your business, and your phone pings. It is a notification from one of your social media apps or a message from your friend. You "quickly" have a look and respond to it. But this can happen ten or twenty times in an hour. In that time, you will have lost half the time you had set aside for your new-business work.

Instead, focus on what you are doing now—wholeheartedly. Turn your phone off. Make sure you will not be hopping up to get a drink or a snack. Sit and truly work for that hour.

When you go online to start researching compound interest rates, *don't* check your email or get lost on an Internet search that eventually finds you watching a video of a giraffe eating breakfast.

THE ENTERPRISING ENTREPRENEUR

You know how it is: you start at one place, and you get side-tracked. Side-tracked is exactly what you will be. Distractions take you to the side of the track you are meant to be on.

You remember that track, right? It's the one you are on to change your life and start your own business. Well, you are not going to get there if you are standing on the side of your track, watching videos of giraffes.

Find a quiet space in which you can work, and focus. Sitting at a table in the middle of a busy kitchen is not going to give you the quiet you need to think clearly, and you do need to think clearly, to be able to run with a thought process and see where it takes you.

You are not planning an outing to the park. You are planning a strategy to start your own business and change your life forever. I think that deserves some dedicated attention, don't you? You will be amazed at what you can achieve in that short time frame, if you don't allow yourself to be distracted.

Focus is not about grim determination and furious writing. It is not a little cartoon character sitting and writing so fervently that there is smoke coming from his pencil. It is about giving yourself a physical and mental space in which to think without distractions.

You need to allow yourself to follow a train of thought without someone asking you something that stops that thought. We all know how, when that happens, you may never get back to where you were before the distraction. What if that thought was *the* thought—*the* solution you had been worrying over, and suddenly it was there and then it was gone?

Don't underestimate the power of allowing yourself to think, to plan, and to use your time wisely. It will always pay dividends and compound into something useful.

If you don't have a space that is out of the way—and many of us don't, as we live with family members who are in and about the house—use headphones to create a "me" space.

THE ENTERPRISING ENTREPRENEUR

You can listen to music while you think and work. There are some great playlists on YouTube for helping with your concentration. And perhaps set up a rule with your family that, when you have your headphones on, you are a no-go zone, unless there is an emergency.

Remember: we are speaking about only an hour a day. The house is not going to fall down, and the children are not going to come to any harm; you can easily put everything in place before you start, to ensure that everyone is fine and no one will need you. An understanding partner can help you, too, as your new venture may well be something that you both need to do, so taking on the family responsibilities for that hour is a gesture can be returned, when they need a little time to think and take a break.

You can also go to a library, as there is always quiet there. The benefit of a library is that they also have an amazing reference section. As does the Internet, though the Internet comes with many side distractions that are absent at the library.

You need to know what you want to do, how you are going to achieve it, and what your steps should be between where you are now and where you want to arrive. Developing all that is not going to happen in a moment. It will take a lot of thought and research.

Focusing there, at the start, will ensure that your road ahead is smoother than it would be otherwise. Put in the effort now, and reap the rewards later.

Focus for Development and Input

Say you have done your planning, created your timeline with its milestones, and started your business. Now your focus is going to be on sustaining what you have started. You will still find that you need to set aside time to think, strategize, and plan as you go along. There will always be something that requires your thinking cap to be firmly on your head.

When you are running your business, every nuance and detail of it requires your focus. It is not going to run itself. You need to keep your finger on the pulse of the whole operation.

Know what is going on in every area, such as:

- ✓ What your customers think about the product and staff
- ✓ Maintaining the product quality
- ✓ Keeping up the production and distribution
- ✓ How to advertise your business

All this needs to be done with the greatest impact at the lowest cost without compromising on quality.

You can see why your business is going to need your focus. Don't go into business half-heartedly. A half-hearted attempt is going to give you a half-hearted result.

By keeping focused on the day-to-day process of your business, you can preempt any problems and find solutions to avoid a problem becoming greater than it needs to. Quick identification of problems and quick solutions save the credibility of your business and will also save you money.

Be focused on what you do, who you employ, what you are putting in, and what you are getting out. Being an entrepreneur is much the same as being a juggler, except you are juggling time, money, products, and clients.

You may say, "But I can't juggle!"

Well, of course you can—if you spend an hour a day learning how to do it. You can do *anything,* if you prioritize your time and give it your focus.

Change

Though being focused is very important, being dogmatic about the direction you are going can be detrimental to your success. Change is necessary in order to flow comfortably in the direction you are meant to go. Understanding this will get you into the right headspace, one that keeps you moving instead of ranting about how things are not going your way.

Since we have spent so much time and effort breathing life into the initial idea, planning how to make it work, and putting that plan into action, we don't want to accept that we need to change course in order to go forward. There is a delightful saying:

The nice thing about hitting your head against a wall is when you stop.

Being flexible within your fixed idea of what you want will take you forward faster. If you keep your initial idea but tweak how you do it or how you sell it to others, you can adapt your plan without throwing it out. You may also find new information that alters the way you look at how you currently do things.

Market trends change, and you need to change with them. Perhaps the target market you thought you were aiming for is not your biggest target market, so you may need to adapt your advertising and marketing to suit the change. If you are not willing to change, you will keep butting up against a brick wall and not move forward. We do not, and cannot, know everything, and only an arrogant person thinks they do—and he is often a fool who fails.

Be ready to accept that you and your business may need to change course in order to move forward. Change will be needed, which may mean reshuffling how you run the business and adapting to ensure that you grow. Just remember: it is *growth* that will make you a success.

Fixation on One Idea Blocks Change

Earlier in the book, I used an analogy of a river flowing. That is exactly what you need to be. Water is an amazing thing. When it encounters an obstacle, it either goes around it, over it, under it, or through it, but it does not allow that obstacle to block its flow.

People say water is destructive. I prefer to think of it as tenacious. It does not know when to quit moving forward. For an entrepreneur, there can be no better way to conduct your business.

If you encounter an obstacle, be water. Go around, under, over, or through it. Water can get through concrete; it can get through rock; it wears away dams over time.

What happens when you are fixated on one idea and refuse to change? Your flow is blocked. You become ice, and ice doesn't break through anything until it melts and becomes water again.

You have to keep in mind that something that may have been right at one time may not be right now or may not work for you in the future. Being dogmatic about something that is clearly not working is as good as giving up and throwing your dreams out the window.

This does not mean you must change direction every time you encounter an obstacle. When you encounter an obstacle or a problem, first try to solve it. Try to find a solution that works within your plan to make it go away or be resolved. Keep trying; keep working at it. Eat away at it, and often it will dissolve.

However, when you fixate on doing things one way and it clearly isn't working, there comes a moment when you are going to have to choose between continuing on a path that's sinking your business or changing your flow and creating a new path forward.

Keep Your Eye on Your End Goal

If you keep your eye on the end goal, you will notice how some slight movements to the left or right as you change your flow will not stop you from reaching your goal. You can afford to be flexible. Being flexible means moving so as not to break. Remember the tree branch when it moves in the wind: it flexes but does not break.

Life will throw the unexpected your way, and you cannot account for every surprise at the start of the journey. As long as you don't lose sight of what you are going to achieve, however, you can always change the way you get there. Make sure you set aside time and money for the unknowns.

While for a while at the beginning you may be stretched tight financially, do what you must do to keep some money set aside. Things happen that you can't foresee, and it will usually take extra money to sort them out. Don't let this small thing be the thing that derails your train.

Perhaps your landlord wants an extra month's rent as deposit. Perhaps you find someone perfect to work for you but know you will need to pay them a bit extra, in order to secure their employ. Or perhaps production costs go up unexpectedly. These small hurdles can have a great impact on your potential success, if you don't have some cash put away for emergencies.

Keeping your eye on the end goal means being fluid and not throwing your hands up in defeat at every small challenge. Learn to change and adapt to new situations. Keep your eye on the end goal. This focus will keep you moving forward, no matter what obstacles come across your path.

Adapt

Not many people have the skill to accept change and adapt accordingly. By being willing to adapt, you open yourself up to new opportunities. Embracing these will move you forward in leaps and bounds.

Accepting change and adapting will allow you to survive any challenge you may encounter. Think of a football player. It is very seldom that they have a straight run across the field to the goal posts. No. Generally, they dodge and weave their way around other players until they get to where they want to be.

That is how you need to be, as well. There is never just one path to the goal. Sometimes, you have to go left; sometimes, you have to go right. Sometimes, you have to jump over other people. But as long as you keep moving forward, those side-steps and jumps will never slow you down. They are simply redirecting your energy in order to advance your progress in a changing environment.

Working hard to find a solution and adapting through flexibility are not opposing forces. They work hand in hand. When you encounter something that isn't working, you will first try to find a solution. I guarantee you, the solution will come from making a change and adapting in some way. Being flexible, changing, and adapting will also cause those around you to see how you are growing through a problem, and they will do the same. You will be leading from the front.

Adapting is not failure. It takes a very strong person to accept that something is not working and then try another way. We are preconditioned as humans to doggedly keep going in the same direction, on the same path, until we get old and retire. That is old-school thinking. While having a good, stable job is a great thing for some people, those of us who have that enterprising entrepreneur within us are never going to be happy in a humdrum, nine-to-five job.

We want to make a change. We want the challenges that come with being in control of our own destinies and lives.

We don't want to work from paycheck to the same old paycheck, waiting for our annual increase. We want to be able to create something that has the potential to grow exponentially.

We want to see our efforts grow like compound interest, which cannot happen in a linear job.

We are the ones who change our lives and write our own futures, because we are the ones who grab our inspiration by the collar and say, "*Yes*! Let's do this!"

We are the ones who are willing to dance on our feet, jump, sidestep, adapt, and change. We overcome the obstacles we face and then make that daring run for the end of the field to score the winning goal for Team Me.

CHAPTER 8

NETWORKING TO BUILD BRIDGES

NETWORKING IS VERY important. I see networking as a bridge. The connections you make carry you from where you are to another place. Whether they are work-based or personal networks, they link us to a wide variety of people who all have something to teach us. They link us from where we didn't know something to where we learn something new. In this way, they are a bridge.

If you look at it in this way, you are on the bank of a river. The place where you want to be, as an entrepreneur, is on the opposite bank. Between the two banks is a raging river that is too rough to swim or row across.

The only way across this river is to build a bridge. Networking is that bridge. It will be one of the things that moves you from where you are to the future you are dreaming about.

Building Bridges Not Walls

We all carry baggage, whether it is emotional baggage from being made to feel not good enough, or baggage from past failures. I am sure it is there. Due to this, people build walls to protect themselves rather than reach out to others by building bridges.

Building walls may protect you from being hurt, but they also protect you from receiving anything. Walls cast shadows and loom above you, blocking your view of what the world is really like, and giving you a skewed view of what is out there.

Trusting others is something you have to learn to do, if you want to run your own business. You have to trust your suppliers to make your product properly. You have to trust your transport company to deliver the product to you on time. And you have to trust your staff to do their best in selling your product to the public.

There is not one instance in business when you can succeed without people interaction. No matter what has happened to you in the past, you need to find a way to get to a point where you realize that bad things happen but not all the time, and that there are bad people out there, but not all people are bad.

It is imperative for your success that you take the risk and climb over those walls you have built. You need to start building bridges between you and other people. It is good for your morale, if nothing else, to meet like-minded people.

The links you make in life, these bridges, are life support systems for you personally and for your business. Your family and friends are your support, when you need to just relax or need some motivation. You cross the bridge, and there they are. If you have a wall built, you will sit alone and feel miserable.

In business, the bridges we build link us to other like-minded people with whom we can share experiences and knowledge and gain support.

Networking for Growth

Through networking, you can also create new contacts and expand your opportunities. You can create a support network and also an expansion network.

I believe in networks and also that you don't ever meet people by chance. They come into your life because you have something to teach them and they have something to teach you. Part of reaching out and building bridges is accepting that not everything will work out perfectly, but that is also okay, as it is just how life works.

I was very fortunate to meet my wife. She and I are very like-minded in what we want from life and what we want to do with our lives.

Meeting my wife's best friend and her husband was also fortunate, as they, like us, were driven to make a difference in the world and become successful doing it. They and my wife understood what I meant when I said we have to try to make a difference, and if we fail, we fail.

If we fail, we can go back to our day-to-day jobs until we find another way of making a difference, and then we will try again. Failing is part of life. You fall, you learn the lesson, you pick yourself up, and you try again. But you do not let it stop you from trying or from reaching out to others and networking, in order to create a greater platform on which to build your dreams.

I'm pleased to say, though, that the business the four of us started—me, my wife, and our two friends—is still going today and is still successful.

How to Create a Network: Personal Networking

For me, I will always start creating a network within my own circles. These are the people whom I already have around me and who know my view point and my dreams. They already understand where I am coming from. I don't have to explain myself to them.

If I fail, they will be there to console me and help me get up and encourage me to try again, so a strong family and friend network is invaluable. When you start going after your goals and dreams, you will find that you lose some people. There is a sifting process that happens.

There are those people who liked you when you were unhappy, because it resonated with their unhappiness—bizarrely. They don't want you to step out of your comfort zone, because then they are alone and doing nothing about changing their own lives in the ways you are.

There are those whom you trust with your dreams and share your ideas with, but they betray you or take your ideas and use them for themselves. I know this is not a common occurrence, but it does happen.

There are those who, because you are making strides in achieving your dreams, blame you for leaving them behind. There are also those who, should you fail, don't want to trust you again.

You have to build up their trust and give it time, but sometimes they don't want to allow that, even though, if the situation was reversed, they would want you to trust them again.

These are the ones you are going to lose, but if people can't walk with you, they become baggage that you either have to drag behind you or leave behind you.

However, the ones who stay by your side are the ones you want anyway. They see your vision, believe in it, and know, even if you fail and fail, eventually you will succeed. They will be there to celebrate with you. Those are the type of people you want in your personal network.

How to Create a Network: Business Networking

In business, you want to seek out two types of people:

1. The Knowledgeable Networkers
2. Newbie Networkers

The Knowledgeable Networkers are people who are experienced in business and who will have many ideas, insights, and experiences that can help you immensely. They have been where you are, they have overcome obstacles you haven't even encountered yet, and they have solutions to problems you are still going to face.

The Newbie Networkers are the ones who, like you, are still finding their feet in the industry. They are good for support, but they are still at the stage where they are learning, which means they are still searching for new and innovative ways to do things. They can offer new, good advice, too.

This network is not quite as valuable as the Knowledgeable Networkers can be for you, when you are starting out. But it can grow, along with you, in expertise and power, so it is good to develop both networks.

Expand Your Network—Expand Your Success

The more you know, the more you grow. This is the same for networking. The more bridges you build, the more rivers you can cross.

How do you expand your network? There are a few ways in which to do it. Some of these are:

* Join allied organizations
* Go to symposiums and conferences
* Use Social Media to your advantage
* Expand your reach and create links with people
* Create an Entrepreneur's blog
* Create podcasts

Join allied organizations

Every field in business has some allied organizations. By joining these organizations, you are immediately in touch with people in your field. They will email you about upcoming events, conferences, webinars, symposiums, and such, at which you could meet other people.

These organizations are also good to be a part of as they always have experienced people on their panels from whom you can gain information around your business or service as well as expertise about new trends and opportunities.

Attend Symposiums and Conferences

It is not good to find out about conferences and similar professional gatherings but then fail to go to them. You have to get out and meet new people. A conference in your field will give you two things:

1. Access to innovative, new ideas
2. An opportunity to meet new people who are in your field.

Use Social Media to Your Advantage

Social media is not just a tool for showing off what you have had for lunch or how cute your dog is. It is a very powerful business tool, if used correctly. There are people whose entire jobs are to create content for businesses' social media pages.

These brand managers post informative and interesting articles and create competitions that link you, the business owner, to potential clients.

Another great social platform for any professional is LinkedIn. It will literally send you suggestions of people who are in similar or the same field as you are in.

Expand Your Reach & Create Links with People

When you are linked to people, through whatever way, create links with them in response. Don't just meet them once and leave it. Contact them, and keep in contact.

Keeping a network active is always going to benefit your business.

Start an Entrepreneur's Blog

Blogging is a great way to get your stories out there into the world. If you think you don't have anything to write about, I can tell you that's not true! There are so many people out there who want to hear how you were working in a nine-to-five job and how you became an entrepreneur.

You will find that your story and journey link you to other entrepreneurs as well as to people who want to start their own businesses but don't yet know how to do it.

Create Podcasts

You can create podcasts and upload them onto Soundcloud or YouTube. What is great about this is that not only are you using your story to motivate others, but they can comment on the podcasts, which gives you new links to people who are interested in your field or business.

About a year and a half ago, I realized it was time for me to expand again. I did my research and decided that the way to go was to get into concept enterprise. This involves working with people, not only on the technical aspects of running a business as an entrepreneur. I began by reaching out to people and letting them know that I was available to speak to groups or students or future entrepreneurs.

I also did some videos that can be seen on YouTube and my social media, plus I have organized my own professional educational seminar.

I am telling you this so you can see that I am putting my feet where I have put my words. Also, to give you some more ideas about how to put these concepts into practice.

But most important, I am doing what I am telling you to do, and it works.

CHAPTER 9

RISK TAKING FOR REWARDS

A LOT OF PEOPLE say they don't like taking risks. However, if you woke up this morning, got up, and walked down the stairs, you took a risk! If you crossed a road on your way to work, you took a risk. If you drove your car, you took a risk. In fact, we all take many risks every day, but as the ones I mentioned are so commonplace, people don't see them as risks.

Risk-taking has been given a bad rap. This is because we have been brainwashed by the media that we all have to succeed, and failure is a terrible thing.

THE ENTERPRISING ENTREPRENEUR

When you move away from this mindset and accept that you will succeed in some things, in others you will fail, and both of those paths are absolutely okay, you won't be so afraid of taking risks.

I have always had a fear of speaking in front of a lot of people. For me, it is a great risk. But I had to let go of that fear and face the fact that I couldn't get my story out there, if I allowed my fear to control me.

So, I had to take that great personal risk. Now that I have overcome it, I can speak in front of people, no problem. I grew because I took the risk.

There are three aspects to risk-taking that I would like to explain to you. These are:

* Taking risks is part of life
* Prepare for success not failure
* Trust yourself to be able to cope

Taking Risks is Part of Life

As we mentioned, risk-taking happens a hundred times a day and should not be something to fear.

We cross roads in faith, believing the cars and trucks will stop for us simply because we are walking on black-and-white stripes painted on the road. We take risks a hundred times a day, so what is so scary about taking a risk on yourself?

I would rather take a risk on myself than on a speeding driver, hoping he'll stop at a pedestrian crossing. I know myself. I know my capabilities. And I know I am committed to what I do and will give it my best shot—every time.

To be an entrepreneur, you have to accept that you are taking a risk. You are putting yourself out there, so you had better be confident in yourself and be confident in what you are going to do.

It is exciting and exhilarating to be your own boss, to make your own decisions, to work hours that suit you and your life, and to have something that can grow as much as you want it to.

There are two type of risks in life:

- ➢ Foreseeable risk
- ➢ Unforeseeable risk

Foreseeable Risks

Foreseeable risks are the sort of risks you know is ahead of you, but you can prepare for them because you know they are coming.

The foreseeable risks are:

- ✓ Giving up a steady job
- ✓ Finances—either using your savings or having to pay back a loan
- ✓ A potentially volatile target market
- ✓ Being your own boss and having to manage yourself and your employees
- ✓ Lack of structured time, since starting a business leaves little time for anything else
- ✓ Finding trustworthy and committed staff
- ✓ Acts of God and Men

Giving up a steady job

Even if you start out working your regular job and running your business, there will come a time when you will have to pick one or the other, as the demands on your time will mean you won't be able to do both.

Giving up a steady job is a daunting prospect when the next paycheck is not guaranteed. But it is a risk you have to take, perhaps the biggest leap of faith in yourself that you will ever make.

By doing this, you are saying to yourself and to the world, "I trust my ability to make this work. I back myself."

Finances—Use your savings or pay back a loan?

Saving money is hard. Then using all your savings to start your own business is also hard, but at the same time it is exciting. It's that start-of-a-roller-coaster-ride feeling. You are excited, but there is a feeling of apprehension, too.

This is where your business plan and research come to the fore. You can feel less stressed about using your savings if you have done your homework and ensured that, even throughout the lean months, you will be able to pay back your loan or have money to live on.

A potentially volatile target market

There is very little you can do about market fluctuations and people being fickle about whatever the latest trend is.

If you have a business that is trend-product related, know that timing is everything. You have to get in while the trend runs, because it won't last. You also need to have your next plan ready to go.

If you have a product that is a necessity in life, like food, drink, or service-related business, you are less at risk, because people will always need these things, so the market for them is more stable.

Being your own boss and managing employees

Being your own boss is one of the greatest perks of being an entrepreneur.

Anyone who has worked at an office has a story about when they had a great idea that would have brought money in or saved the company money, but they were not allowed to run with it.

Or a story about a horrible boss who wouldn't give them time off for their child's ball game or ballet concert. The great thing about being your own boss is that you can work your job around your life.

That's a plus. The *risk* is that you don't put in enough time and your business suffers because of it.

Being an entrepreneur means working more but working smarter, and therefore reaping a compound-effect interest on your efforts put in, both financially and personally.

Lack of structured time

No matter what business you are in, there are going to be times when things go crazy. Something needs urgent attention, or you suddenly have a run on your product and need to get more manufactured quickly. When this happens, whatever else is going on in your life has to take a back seat.

Knowing that these situations are going to arise means you can forewarn your family and work around them.

Crises and rushes are always temporary, or they should be. If they become the norm, however, you need to look at your business structure and get more staff.

Finding trustworthy staff

On that note, finding good, trustworthy, and motivated staff is not easy. There can be a lot of staff turnover, which is why I thought up the incentive scheme for my chapati kiosks.

A staff member who has a vested interest in your business will put in more effort and focus than one who is working simply for the paycheck. Work out some sort of incentive scheme. It could be financial or a weekend away, or have them work towards a share of owning the branch of that business one day.

Another point on staff: treat them decently. Pay them a decent wage, and treat them with respect. Without them, your business cannot run. Acknowledge them for the great help they are, but also set a clear set of rules and be sure they know about from the outset.

Remember that you can be a good boss, but you cannot be a good boss and a buddy. Keep the line clear and the rules are simple. And be nice!

When I worked in the bank, before we started our business, I was working in a CV kiosk one day, and this very smart-looking man came up to me. He looked right through me, like I wasn't even there. He had to speak to me, but he acted as if I was some small, insignificant bug. Then and there I promised myself I would be successful one day *and* I would never treat people like that man had treated me, or make anyone feel as he had made me feel.

I knew, at that moment, that I needed to create awareness in employers and in people in general to treat staff and others decently.

Unforeseeable Risks: Acts of God and Men

Insurance companies call floods, hurricanes, fires, and other natural disasters Acts of God. It is important to insure your business against all the risks that you can.

The Acts of Men are theft, vandalism, arson, looting, etc. When you have a business, insurance is a must. It is a grudge payment, but should you need it, you will be thankful that you paid your premiums each month.

The unforeseeable risks are:

- ✓ Unforeseeable changes in the economy
- ✓ Operational problems
- ✓ Your customers
- ✓ A new competitor
- ✓ The big "?"

Unforeseeable changes in the economy

I understand the economy, but I don't want to be ruled by its daily ups and downs. Those do not impact my life of business.

However, if you are, for example, importing a product, and there is a flux in the exchange rate between your country and the one you are importing from, you can suddenly find yourself having to pay out a lot more than you did last week for the same products.

In the same way, import and export taxes will vary. In certain businesses, you need to be cognizant of outside economic and political influences that will affect your cash flow.

Operational problems

Nothing ever goes 100% smoothly. Staff get sick unexpectedly, machines break, imports don't arrive in time, and many other things occur on a regular basis that can have an impact on your business. Whilst these are unforeseeable in their entirety, you can plan "What If" scenario solutions and put them in place.

Some examples of these are:

➢ *What if* my staff member goes off sick for a week—can I step in? Or do I need to have another person on standby?

➢ *What if* my import gets stuck in port, and I can't get it delivered for a week? I can ensure that I have enough surplus stock to cover that in my storeroom.

➢ *What if* my truck is stolen whilst out on a delivery? Ensure that you have insurance to cover the loss.

➢ *What if* the machine making my ice cream breaks? I can have another one on standby from the supplier, who will deliver it within an hour.

You can put countermeasures in place for some of the possible eventualities, but not for all of them. When there is nothing you can do, be honest with your customers and get cracking on fixing the problem.

Don't tell a lie to cover the problem. Be straight with them. They will either accept it or not accept it, but at least you will be playing open cards with them.

Be a person of integrity in all your business dealings. And, it goes without saying, in your personal life, too.

Remember the compound principle? It works on integrity, truth, decency, and kindness, but it also works on lies, dishonestly, deceit, and malice. What you sow you will reap. In compound interest.

Your customers

People are fickle, as I mentioned in the foreseeable risks section. But they need to be added to this section as well, because they can be an unforeseeable risk.

From one day to the next, your customer base could dry up. That is why I always suggest a Plan B. What else can you do with your product or services? Who else can you market to?

Again, you can try and create a "What If" solution, but often you just have to think on your feet.

A new competitor

So, your business is doing well, you are finally making money, and life is good. Then someone else opens a similar store or starts a similar business in your area.

Suddenly, your customer base is halved, if you are lucky. If you are unlucky, the customers will flock to that other service or store, because it is new.

This is something to be aware of. With staff, a restraint of trade agreement should be signed, in order to prevent their leaving and opening the same business next door. Other than that, you have to find your path around that obstacle if it happens.

The big "?"

This is the real unforeseeable risk—the one you would never have thought of in ten years.

It could be a flood, a hurricane, a fire, or an earthquake. It could be your needing to sell your business because of a family crisis. The big "?" is the one unforeseeable risk that you will just have to deal with as it happens.

Prepare for Success, Not Failure

If you prepare well, your failure rate will be lower. However, accept that all the preparation in the world is not going to stop challenges coming your way.

Prepare as well as you can, adapt where you need to, and learn from every experience. By preparing well, you are invariably decreasing your risks, decreasing your change of failure, and increasing your chances for success.

Ariana Huffington of *The Huffington Post* says that failure is not the opposite of success; it is a stepping stone to success. That resonates with how I see failure. It has a bad rap! It is simply a hard lesson learned, but a valuable one nonetheless. We fall, we fail, we cry, we get up—a little wiser—and we try again, knowing more than we did the last time we tried.

Whilst we must accept that we cannot succeed at everything, we cannot go into any venture, relationships, or job thinking we are going to fail. Yes, as I have described, you can preempt certain risks, but then you have to go into your entrepreneurial venture with a positive attitude and prepare for the success you are going to make of your venture.

Work as if you are not going to fail, but prepare anyway. This is not being fatalistic. It is being *realistic*. If you prepare for risks that you can prepare for, they will not knock you off your feet as they would, if you hadn't prepared for them.

Trust Yourself to Be Able to Cope

Tying in with the chapter on backing yourself, you also have to trust that you will be able to cope with any challenge life throws at you. Trust in yourself. Believe, even if you don't know the solution, you have the skills and tenacity to find it.

I have a story that ties in nicely with this. At the time we started our business, I was working for the Digital Federal Credit Union, which is credit union bank here in Boston. How I got the job at this bank is an important lesson on trusting yourself and backing yourself.

I applied to this bank for a job four times. I was turned down each time. That did not deter me, as I knew what I wanted to do, which was to work at this bank.

I decided on another tack. I stopped in at the bank and went to speak to the manager. Whilst the job post continued to be offered online, I had had enough of online applications. I thought, if I could get the manager to give me and interview, I would at least have a shot at getting the job.

There was a temporary manager on duty that day, as the usual manager was away on leave. I told her that I had applied four times for an interview and had been rejected all four times. I believed, at very least, I should be given an interview.

THE ENTERPRISING ENTREPRENEUR

She listened to my story and said she would give me an interview the next day. I was so happy! Even if I didn't get the job, at least this person had given me a chance after all those rejections.

I wanted to get into banking so badly at that stage of my life. That particular woman interviewed me and then she hired me. It worked out well, as she became the manager of that branch, so she took me under her wing and trained me.

Working in the bank taught me a great deal. The manager taught me how to approve loans, and she put me in charge of teams as a leader, even though I was on a lower pay grade than other team members.

That is one of the things I have been impressed with in America. I have been made to feel I can be a leader. I can be in charge. I can make changes that will matter to people. Things are not done that way in my home country, so I am grateful to be here and given that platform on which to grow.

The reason I got to be a team leader above these other people was because I was motivated, enthusiastic, and keen to learn anything about banking that they would teach me. I knew it was a good opportunity, and I was not going to squander it. I used it to develop myself and my skills.

Whenever I didn't know something, I would go to the manager and say to her, "Please, teach me about this, or show me how to do that."

One thing I learned is that someone who backs themselves and is willing to learn is easy to teach. Through her, I learned a lot about banking and how it works in America. I also learned how to do many applications, which stood me in good stead for when I opened our business.

ଓଓଓ

THE ENTERPRISING ENTREPRENEUR

You never know everything there is to know when you start a business. Trust yourself to be able to cope, to be resourceful enough to find answers, and to be tenacious enough to work around obstacles. Then you are well on your way to becoming an enterprising entrepreneur.

CHAPTER 10

5 GOLDEN PRINCIPLES

THERE ARE CERTAIN things that matter to me, both within myself and about the people I surround myself with. These are what I call my M 5 Golden Principles for Life. These are:

- ✳ Integrity
- ✳ Action
- ✳ Leadership
- ✳ Take Risks
- ✳ Network

Integrity

Integrity is at the top of my list, because all the other decent human traits fall under its umbrella. If you have integrity, you will be honest. You will treat people well. You will always give your best and strive to be the very best version of yourself that you can possibly be.

Integrity is not just about who you are. It is about how you treat others in the same way you want to be treated. It is about being honest, fair, kind, and ethical. The easy route in life is to be dishonest and use people for what you can get out of them. To me, integrity is something that you work on every day and is the most important principle for life.

Action

Without action, we all become stagnant rivers. Action is our fluidity, the water in our souls, and the fire in our veins.

Actions take us from here to anywhere we want to go. When you combine action and integrity, you get a very powerful force in a person that creates change and success out of life.

Be a person of action. Don't allow your days to sift through your fingers like sand. Act today, and start working on creating the future you want to live in.

Leadership

Leadership is important to me because it is the main way you can influence people and teach them.

You have to be a leader who has something to teach. I have worked hard to hone my leadership skills and admire them in a person, knowing that they are worth working on.

Good leaders become successful because they are people of action and integrity. Good leaders make good bosses and good business people for those same reasons.

Take Risks

If you don't take risks, you will never do something spectacular. Nothing ventured, nothing gained.

You may limit the risks by preparing for as many eventualities or "what ifs" as you can, but try always to have resources at your disposal to cover you for the rest.

Don't let fear of failure stop you from stepping into success.

Network

Networking is the link that binds all business people. Active networking is not only vital, but it is good for us as people. Through networking, we create new contacts, gain knowledge we didn't have before, and establish a support system that we can rely on.

അരുരുരു

These five golden principles are what I base my entrepreneurial skills. They are how I run my business and live my life. They have proved to be gold to me. That is why I am sharing them with you. Find your own five golden principles for life and then live them to their fullest.

CONCLUSION

ANYONE CAN BE an enterprising entrepreneur, but you have to want it. First you must dream it, then plan it, and truly work it.

It is possible! And I can tell you, I have never been happier than I am being my own boss and living my dream.

I want everyone who wants to be an entrepreneur to feel empowered by my message and my advice. I feel this is the time for all entrepreneurs everywhere to shine.

If you have the desire to be an entrepreneur, know that it takes long hours, hard work, and lots of planning. Know that it is not always easy, but it is very much worth it.

Write your lists. Work out all the details of what you need to do to get you from where you are to where you want to be. Figure out your essential steps.

Then, create a timeline with achievable milestones. Work out your finances and what you are going to need to get you to the point of being able to open your business.

Plan well, network a lot, and don't get knocked off course. Adapt, change, and work around obstacles. Don't forget to ask for help when you need it!

From one enterprising entrepreneur to another—You've got this! I believe in your ability to succeed.

ACKNOWLEDGMENTS

DOING SOMETHING with what you know is what truly makes the difference.

I would like to first of all acknowledge God. He is the reason I am who I am. I give Him all the Glory and Honor for everything in my life.

I am so blessed to have great friends and family who have helped me become the person I am. These people deserve heartfelt thanks and appreciation. Thank you for being part of my life.

A tremendous thank you goes to my team at Concept Enterprises. I deeply appreciate my wife, Loyce Kayongo, who is my worthy partner and adviser. I am greatly honored to be your friend and husband in this journey of life. To our son, we love you and thank you for providing us with endless joy, happiness, and gratitude to God.

Great thanks to Adrian Braka, my Vice President of Operations. Thank you for helping our organization make a difference globally.

Enormous thanks to my strategic partners around the world, who are helping me advance my mission to aid entrepreneurs by assisting them to discover who they truly are and to transform employees into enterprising entrepreneurs.

Special thanks go to Mr. Peter Kimbowa, the founder of the CEO Summit and your honorable wife, Mrs. Kimbowa, for the strategic advice.

I express my respect, love, and gratitude for my mother, Faridah Natoolo, and my father, Richard M. Nsereko. I could never have picked better parents in the world. Your tough love, relentless advice, wisdom, and support have helped me be who I am.

ABOUT THE AUTHOR

BRIAN H. KAYONGO is the Enterprising Entrepreneur. He started his first business on the streets of Kampala when he was just a boy, and he now owns a successful home-care business in Boston.

This book is his story, his journey from being that boy who had a dream to own his own business to the entrepreneur and business owner he is today. He hopes to inspire other people to follow their dreams and achieve their goals, as he did.

The Enterprising Entrepreneur is a book for anyone running their own business or anyone who wants to start their own business.

Brian's story, experiences, and wisdom on business and life are laid bare on the pages of *The Enterprising Entrepreneur*.